THE JOY OF THE GOSPEL

THE JOY
OF THE GOSPEL

Meditations for Young People

Cardinal Carlo Maria Martini

Archbishop of Milan

Translated
by
James McGrath

A Liturgical Press Book

THE LITURGICAL PRESS
Collegeville, Minnesota

Cover design by Mary Jo Pauly.

This book was published in Italian as *La Gioia del Vangelo,* copyright
© 1988 Edizioni Piemme S.p.A., Via del Carmine 5, 15033 Casale Mon-
ferrato (AL), Italy.

	3	4	5	6	7	8	9

Library of Congress Cataloging-in-Publication Data

Martini, Carlo M.
    [Gioia del Vangelo. English]
    The joy of the Gospel : meditations for young people / Carlo Maria
Martini ; translated by James McGrath.
        p.   cm.
    ISBN 0-8146-2126-0
    1. Retreats for youth. 2. Spiritual exercises. 3. Turning water
into wine at the wedding at Cana (Miracle)—Meditations. 4. Bible.
N.T. Mark—Meditations. 5. Youth—Religious life. 6. Spiritual
life—Catholic Church. 7. Catholic Church—Doctrines. I. Title.
BX2376.Y73M3713 1994
242'.63—dc20   93—37441
                                                              CIP

Contents

PART II
Quantum Leaps on the Christian Educational
Journey: School of the Word on the Gospel
according to Mark

Preface

This volume contains two collections of meditations on the word of God given by Cardinal Carlo Maria Martini, archbishop of Milan, to young people from the Ambrosian Church in connection with the diocesan pastoral program, "God Instructs His people."

The first collection consists of a course of spiritual exercises given evenings during Lent 1988—from March 21 to March 25 in the cathedral—to commemorate the centenary of the death of St. John Bosco and also to prepare for the third World Youth Day, celebrated in all the local Churches on Palm Sunday, March 27.

The title of the exercises, "Do whatever he tells you," repeats the title of Pope John Paul II's message to youths and to all the young people of the world. The Holy Father hoped that listening to the words spoken by Mary at the wedding feast of Cana would promote a deeper probing of the mystery of our Lady, which would help us understand what it truly means to believe in the love of God and to live by this love.

In response to the Holy Father's invitation, the meditations composed by the archbishop in the exercises are a beginning for contemplating the mystery of Jesus, the Lord of our life, of history, and of Mary.

The second collection presents the meditations of the archbishop to students in the monthly meetings of the "School of the Word," which for several years he had given to young people in the various pastoral zones of the diocese.

In accordance with the practical suggestions in the third part of the pastoral letter, "God Instructs His People," the Schools of the Word were encouraged to read in the Gospel of St. Mark the excerpts which best show the difficult moments of separation, of crises of growth which the stages of conversion imply, and which bring light on the journey that Jesus brings to fulfillment for his apostles as he leads them to faith in him and his mystery. From this comes the title of the collection, "Advances in quality on the road of christian education."

"The joy of the gospel" beautifully indicates, it would seem, the cornerstone of all of the cardinal's meditations. We are able to perceive this joy in these words which come from his heart, as if they were a communication of his own faith experience and his pastoral life, leaping out from his contemplative heart. Young people have felt themselves known and understood in the midst of their (sometimes unexpressed) questions, in their fragility, in their difficulties and doubts; they have felt understood and helped.

It seems helpful to point out at least two points on which the archbishop insists. They are reminders for each of us, young people and adults, men and women, lay persons and priests, and none of these have been left out. We must make these points of reflection and examine them beginning with our personal, concrete experiences and those of our communities.

First, at the beginning of the exercises the cardinal stresses that we all have need "to be more deeply rooted in contemplation," we need to "give space to the Holy Spirit within us," by growing in gospel faith and by building up community. Contemplation, indeed, is at the root of every real choice in life and of every Christian action; everything that we can say about divine reality to our brothers and sisters comes to us from contemplation and this is sparked in us by listening to the word of God, which puts us in contact with Jesus, the living Word. It is necessary to bind ourselves seriously to meditative and loving reflection on the Scriptures, on the *lectio divina* (sacred reading) as lived within the framework of the Church, in its living tradition and teaching. *Lectio divina* is not a luxury because it is the exercise, or the instrument, by means of which the Christian learns to know the Bible and as a result to confront realistically his or her own existence with the Word.

This reminder indicates, in our opinion, a personal concern. If contemplation has not taken root, Christian communities risk being highly organized, programmed, efficiency-oriented, and as a result easily open to quarrels, to self-justification, to unending discussions.

Second, the Cardinal emphasizes the joy of the gospel. At other times he had already referred to and emphasized that the joy of the gospel is an "inexpressible something" which pervades the entire life of the baptized person, which is balance for everything, and which corresponds with the spirituality of Mary. The Pope also recently recalled this point in a discourse to the Roman Curia on Christmas 1987 by affirming the necessity for the Church always to join the "Petrine principle" with the "Marian principle."

Here above all we take note of the archbishop's concern to make us understand that the joy of the gospel has its greatest revelation in the cross and becomes the *joy of the cross*, which is the highest expression of the love of the Father, in Jesus, for humankind. The cardinal insists on the theme of the cross, and is concerned lest anyone might wish to live the Christian life by prescinding from that reality. The Church is an outpouring of the heart of Christ which was broken by his death, and the Holy Spirit continuously introduces the baptized person into the heart of this mystery. Until we have made this truth part of us, and until we have listened to, and come face-to-face with, the theme of the cross for our life, our communities will not be successful in exploding into a dynamism of love.

These points of emphasis do not prevent the archbishop from showing, in addition to this firmness of thought, a constant and serene optimism for the Church and for the human beings, since from his words and prayers there emerges a profound and most tender devotion to Mary, the Virgin of listening and of joy, the Mother of instruction in the faith, the image of the Church on pilgrimage.

We feel sure that this small volume could become the *vade mecum* for many young people desirous of growing to maturity in the faith, for many educators, and for all those faithful who desire to reach a coherent Christian life by undertaking to give testimony to evangelical conduct and to the teachings of the Church.

The archbishop could not have given us a more beautiful gift in this Marian year and in this pastoral biennium on education. He shows once again his pastoral care and sure guidance for the pilgrimage of our Church through his example and teaching.

Fr. Franco Agnesi

"Do whatever he tells you"

(John 2:5)

The exercise
of *lectio divina*

Introduction

In the pastoral letter to the diocese for the biennium 1987–89, under the title "God Instructs His People," I wrote that the Holy Spirit—he who "has spoken through the prophets" and has inspired the Scriptures—speaks also to us today. And I added that training for listening to the interior Teacher must come about by the exercise of prayerful meditation on the word of God, by *lectio divina* ("God Instructs His People," part 1, no. 19).

I would like now, by way of introduction, to point out the method for *lectio divina* which I proposed in the exercises for young people, recalling the incident at Cana treated in St. John's Gospel. I propose then to compare his account with the classic method of prayer which used the triple formula memory, intellect, will.

Lectio divina is a gradual approach to the biblical text and harks back to the ancient method used by the Fathers, who in their turn referred to rabbinical usage.

The classical subdivision into memory, intellect, will, is very old and was developed especially by St. Augustine, at least as far as the reference to memory is concerned. Somewhat later this triad became synonymous with a meditative process of reflecting on the Scriptures or on one of the truths of the faith.

I shall also briefly recall the method of "evangelical contemplation," a term as a rule used to indicate the manner of meditating on a passage of the gospel; we have a good example of this in the *Spiritual Exercises* of St. Ignatius Loyola, who at the start of the Second Week speaks of "contemplation" because for the work of the intellect he generally replaces an existential and prayerful involvement with a scene from the gospel.

All of this will be useful in understanding better the specific characteristic of *Christian prayer*.

Lectio divina

The patristic method of *lectio divina* is very simple and I always recommend it to young people as a means of entering into prayer. Fundamentally it envisions three important steps or successive periods:

The *lectio* consists in reading and re-reading a selection from Scripture, placing in prominence its significant elements. That is why I advise reading with pen in hand, underlining the words that are striking, or calling attention with graphic symbols to words, actions, subjects, sentiments expressed, or the key word.

In this way our attention is stimulated, the intellect, imagination, and emotions are moved so that they make the best-known passage appear to be new. Though I have been reading the gospel for many years, every time I take it up again in my hand I discover some new facets especially by means of this method of *lectio*.

This initial work can take very little time if we are open to the Spirit: the excerpt read is put in a broader context, whether it is related to nearby verses, or to the same book, or to the whole Bible, so as to understand what it means.

The *meditatio* is reflection on the lasting values in the text. While in the *lectio* I am taking in the relevant historical, geographical, and even cultural facts of the passage, here the question comes up: What is this saying *to me*? In reference *to our day* what message from the passage is conclusively proposed as the living word of God? How am I motivated by the permanent values that lie behind the actions, the words, the subjects?

Contemplatio can be expressed and explained only with difficulty. It consists in lingering with love on the text, by passing from the text and from the message to the contemplation of him who speaks on every page of the Bible: Jesus, Son of the Father, the Sender of the Holy Spirit.

Contemplatio is adoration, praise, silence in the presence of him who is the ultimate object of my prayer, Christ the Lord, conqueror of death, the revealer of the Father, the absolute mediator of salvation, the giver of the joy of the gospel.

In practice these three parts are not really distinct; however, the division is useful for those who need to start or to resume this exercise. Our praying is like a red thread that links up the days one to the other so that from the same text of the Scriptures on one day we stop with *meditatio* whereas on another day we quickly go right to *contemplatio.*

The threefold distinction nevertheless expresses almost in an elementary way the compelling force of *lectio divina,* which in one of my books I explained with all its complexities. In fact, these complexities include eight progressive steps: *lectio, meditatio, oratio, contemplatio, consolatio, discretio, deliberatio, actio.*

At this point I think it worthwhile to explain these briefly.

Oratio is the first prayer that comes from meditation: Lord, make me understand the permanent values I am missing in the text, grant me the gift of understanding what your message means for my life.

At a certain point this prayer is concentrated on adoration and on the contemplation of the mystery of Jesus, of the countenance of God. The *oratio* can be expressed also in a request for forgiveness, for light or as an offering prayer.

Consolatio is very important for our journey in prayer and St. Ignatius of Loyola speaks of it many times in his *Spiritual Exercises.* Without this component prayer looses its salt, its taste. *Consolatio* is the joy of prayer, it is experiencing intimately a taste for God, for things about Christ. It is a gift which is ordinarily produced in the context of *lectio divina* even though obviously the Holy Spirit is free to confer the gift when he desires.

Only from *consolatio* come the courageous choices of poverty, chastity, obedience, fidelity, and forgiveness, because it is the place, the atmosphere, proper to the great interior choices. Whatever does not come from this gift of the Spirit lasts but a short time and may easily be the result of moralism which we impose on ourselves.

Discretio expresses even more clearly the vitality of *consolatio*. In fact, through taste for the gospel, through a sort of spiritual scent for things of Christ, we become sensitive to all that is gospel and all that is not. This is an important discernment because we are not called finally to observe the commandments, but rather to follow Jesus. And following him is not immediately evident in the daily choices we make if we do not, so to speak, enter into the mind of Jesus, if we have not tasted his poverty, his cross, the humility of his crib, his forgiveness.

This capacity to discern in the ordinary emotions and movements of the heart, this evangelical hallmark is a gift so great that St. Paul begged for it for all the faithful: ''And this is my prayer: that your love may increase ever more and more in knowledge and every kind of perception, to discern what is of value, so that you may be pure and blameless for the day of Christ'' (Phil 1:9-10; Rom 12:2).

Today the Church has extreme need for *discretio* because our decisive choices are not only about what is good and what is bad (do not kill, do not steal), but about what is *better* for the pilgrimage of the Church, for the world, for the good of people, for youths, for children.

Deliberatio is the next step. From the interior experience of consolation or desolation, we learn to discern and, therefore, to *decide* according to God.

If we carefully analyze vocational choices, we notice that they have, maybe unconsciously, this progression. The vocation, in fact, is a decision which begins with a feeling that God has to be felt and with the practical wisdom gained therefrom according to the gospel precepts.

Deliberatio, like *discretio,* is also nurtured in particular by means of the dynamism of *lectio divina.*

Actio finally is the mature fruition of the complete journey. *Lectio* and *actio,* that is, biblical reading and action, are not by any means two parallel lines.

We do not read Scripture to have the strength to carry out what we have decided! On the contrary, we read and we meditate so that correct decisions are born and the consoling strength of the Spirit might help us to put them into practice.

This is not a question, as we so often think, of praying more to do better, but of praying more to understand what I must do and to be able to do it starting from the interior choice.

Its relationship with memory, intellect, will

By examining the terms of the patristic methodology of *lectio divina,* we see that they are in perfect harmony with the Augustinian terms of memory, intellect, will.

Memory consists in recalling, in the case of biblical meditation, a selection of Scripture or an episode or a verse of one of the psalms.

Reference was made to memory and not to *lectio* for the simple reason that in earlier times there was no abundance of books and if a text was heard once it was necessary to remember it. The work of memorizing, among other things, puts one in contact with the vastness of the text in its thousands of ramifications. True memory, therefore, correctly understood, reflects not only on the items found in the biblical passage but recalls other related subjects that happen to come to mind. Then, for those who know the Bible—and every Christian ought to know at least some part of it—there is not a word which is not connected with others. We reflect on the deeds and sayings of Jesus, on references to the Prophets, on some verses of the psalms, and enlarge on them by recalling from memory all the analogous texts.

Today, to do this, we use a concordance. In reality it is a real exercise in memory, another way of expressing the importance of the *lectio;* it is, if you will, a going back to the events *with the heart,* as Mary did.

The term *memory* invites us to understand better that *lectio* means not only recalling facts in the Bible but also other incidents of life similar to the excerpt that we are reading.

Intellect corresponds to *meditatio* and is the search to comprehend the meaning of events. Memory is not enough, understanding is necessary. "Do you not yet understand or comprehend?" Jesus said, ". . . And do you not remember when I broke the five loaves for the five thousand, how many wicker baskets full of fragments you picked up? . . . Do you not yet understand?" (Mark 8:17-21).

Jesus gives an invitation to recall, an invitation to the memory, to the *lectio,* and then he gives an invitation to understand the deeds, to comprehend their meaning.

Will designates everything in a person that is self-gift, love, and finally also prayer as an expression of affection, of enthusiasm, of desire. The will is, in the classical form, the *oratio* and *contemplatio* according to the form we are following here.

The classical method of prayer is finally a different way of looking at the dynamism of *lectio divina* by considering it less as *lectio* and more as objective facts and sayings which are recalled.

Evangelical contemplation

Evangelical contemplation, about which St. Ignatius Loyola spoke in the Second Week of *Spiritual Exercises,* is simply an abbreviation of much of what we said about the patristic method and the classical subdivision, with greater insistence on the theme of prayer-contemplation, with preference given to the skill and to the course of prayer.

Little by little, questions from the *lectio* and the *meditatio* come ever more quickly, while the need to be in the presence of mystery, by praising and adoring, and to taste the presence of Christ increases.

Ignatius speaks of "seeing," "hearing," "touching," "tasting," and "smelling," permitting us to be involved in contemplation even with spiritual senses (*Spiritual Exercises*, nos. 122–125).

The universal dynamism of knowledge

One final note. The methods of prayer we have considered are interrelated because they show the universal dynamism of knowledge.

A person, in fact, starts with *experience*, with having contact with things; and the *lectio*, like the *memory*, are the experience of Christ who lays the foundation and controls all realities.

From experience, then, there comes forth, in the course of human knowledge, *intuition* or the interpretative hypothesis, the understanding of the accumulated data; it is the moment of the *meditatio*, of *understanding*.

The cognitive action then tends to broaden into a choice, an involvement of the heart, a surrender; it is the *contemplatio*, the *will*, with all that comes therefrom.

It seems interesting to me to stress that prayer does not cause a renewal, when speaking of the dynamic of the relationship to the word of God, of the main dynamic for human actions.

Particular characteristics of Christian prayer

Naturally the Spirit guides our prayer in different ways and each individual must search out his or her own prayer methodology, but especially one must search for the way which best corresponds to the way one is living.

The rich patristic and classical terminology emphasizes therefore a common experience in Christian history which has characteristics that are sufficiently precise.

We cannot for this reason confuse Christian prayer with meditations of Hindus, Buddhists, or Transcendentalists; we must not confuse it with the various methods of prayer which are being proposed in our time because Christian prayer has as its base the *lectio,* the *memory,* which is the fact of Christ.

Ours is Christian prayer because it starts with Christ.

At certain moments it can attain an undelineated form: the Risen Christ is present without my contemplating him with mental images. But fundamentally—and I stress this—Christian meditation is a movement of the Spirit and is always associated with Christ Jesus, it is even a participation in the prayer of Jesus to the Father.

An interesting problem arises here relative to the relationship between prayer, the so-called Christic prayer, and the prayer of other religions.

Without doubt there are other forms of authentic prayer from which we can learn, and yet it is very difficult to understand them until we have passed through a serious and profound way of Christian prayer, and as long as we have not uncovered the precious pearl which is the mystery of Jesus.

Whoever has done this, with untiring energy and with gratitude to the Lord above all, since prayer is a gift, will be able then to reap whatever is correct and true in the prayer of other religions.

"To everyone who has, more will be given, but from the one who has not, even what he has will be taken away" (Luke 19:26). To everyone who has the true sense of Christic prayer, will be given to understand the other forms of prayer; from anyone who does not have it, will surely be taken away that bit of prayer which he has because he will confuse it with a kind of interior quiet which changes life so little and risks being the cultivation of one's own idols, the worship of one's self.

I remember an old Buddhist monk, more than eighty years old, who told me during my visit to the monastery in Hong Kong that we are searching for the nothing (*nada*), the scope of our life is the nothing (*nada*).

What was he trying to say? Is his true prayer and what relationship does it have with ours?

If we have the clarity of the ongoing dynamism of Christic prayer, it can be important, as Church, to establish the value of meditation without object, the meaning of the encounter with nothing.

Christic prayer is surrender, *actio*, it is being crucified with Christ, being given to the poorest.

When we are deprived of the light of Christ, the forms of prayers, perhaps beautiful, of other religions are dangers and they pose the risk of becoming mental self-justification, a closing in on one's own choices, self-legitimation. And there is nothing worse on the ascetical journey, or on the so-called spiritual journey, than self-satisfaction.

I am thinking here of persons who pray, pray much, and yet succeed in always doing what they want, in legitimating their own opinions without ever taking the Church seriously or doing justice to truth. Perhaps they have not been helped by becoming truly excited in *lectio divina*, by passing from the experience of meditative reflection to contemplation and to the successive stages which, through the power of the Holy Spirit, transform the word of God lived in life, to evangelical action.

PART I

ONE

The joy of the Gospel

Why these Exercises?

I wish to extend my most cordial greetings to all here present and to all those who are listening on radio as they have gathered in groups in the various churches of the diocese. It is both a wonderful gift from the Lord and a duty for us who are here as well as for those who are physically separated from us to live in a union of prayer.

Three principle motives influenced me to propose to you that there be five successive evenings of reflection and meditation.

The most important motive is the centenary of St. John Bosco, the friend of young people. At one time consideration was given to the possibility of bringing the corpse of the saint to this cathedral, with the thought that with the relics present his message might be heard again.

In any case, Father Bosco is spiritually present, especially with his message of joy: ''Laetare et bene facere''—rejoice and do good. Through his intercession we ask the Lord for the gift of understanding that message of joy which the saint knew how to bring in so efficacious a way to so many young people in his time and even to carry it still today to the entire world.

The second motive is the preparation for World Youth Day which will be celebrated next Sunday and which we shall anticipate in the Saturday vigil Mass with traditional ceremonial.

We wish to be united with the intentions of the Pope and, to achieve this goal, the title of these Exercises repeats the invitation proposed by His Holiness for Youth Day: "Do what he tells you" (John 2:5).

That saying, as you know, is found in the Cana incident, and is transmitted to us in St. John's Gospel. In that episode Mary works for the joy of the guests, for the joy of the couple, for the joy of the people there, and Jesus works for the joy of humankind.

Our exercises will have as their principle theme the question which will be addressed even in this first meditation, but which will also be taken up in the next evenings: What makes my joy fall short? And what increase in joy does the Lord desire to give me for the life which he has in store for me?

The question will have to come out of our hearts. My joy is disturbed by so many personal concerns, by so many things in society—I think of the very sad occurrence in Belfast, for example, of the two soldiers killed by the people—by so many problems in the community.

Lord, how do you wish to infuse into us your strength, your grace, so that we can serve the joy and peace of our neighbors?

The third motive for which I have asked your commitment to these exercises is my utter conviction that it is necessary for all of us to have a more deeply rooted contemplation. We need to enter more into ourselves, to listen in our hearts to the word of God, to look again courageously at the interior troubles that interfere with our joy and to lay them open to the medicine of the word of the Lord. We need to give space to the Holy Spirit within us, in order to act in a more even and more persevering way, to be workers for peace, to overcome our own restlessness and that of our communities, our quarrelsomeness, fears, and prejudices.

Today, at this particular time in the Church, we need above all a greater rootedness in contemplation.

We often hear about the weakness of our modern youths; yet we wish to admit that all of us, the younger and those not so young, are weak and are the more so to the extent that we are less rooted in our faith. And we are so little rooted in the faith because we do not sufficiently persevere in silently listening to the Word.

What is the Lord then asking each of us during these evenings? He is asking, it seems to me, above all for four commitments:

1. *Silence,* which will have its peak in the ten minutes of silence which will follow my suggestions on the Word.

Try to live these moments as the most precious and richest of the evening. That time will not be meaningless if from it springs amazement and respect for the coming of the Holy Spirit who wishes to invade our hearts.

2. *Listening* attentively to the word of God proclaimed in the gospel, listening to my reflection on the text and the final thought of Father Bosco.[1]

3. *Perseverance* against fatigue because the exercise we want to carry out is tiresome and demands victory over ourselves, especially against cold, sleep, noise, nervousness, anxiety.

4. Finally the Lord asks us to *pray* with him by first listening to the Word, then speaking with him and Mary, our Mother, and finally returning to the Father telling him about ourselves, the society in which we live, our own little joy, about what we need, and what we would like to have.

The event at Cana

John the Evangelist has the unique ability to concentrate in a few lines a lot of signs and meaningful thoughts by bringing together in a single text the substance of all the others. Thus if we learn to probe deeply into a single episode we will be able to understand all the rest of the Fourth Gospel and of the history of salvation.

[1] Every evening a Salesian father concluded the meeting by updating some teaching of St. John Bosco.

Let us begin, very simply, to re-read the excerpt about Cana which you have listened to in order to understand it in its fullness, as if we were on the top of a mountain contemplating a panorama.

Most of all we must keep in mind that the account is much more full of meaning that we are prepared for. If it had been Mark, for example, who gave us this account it would have been limited to something like this: "While Jesus was found at a wedding banquet, wine was needed and Jesus changed water which was there into wine; everybody drank it and was satisfied." These few words are adequate to give the "meat" of the matter.

If John, on the other hand, preferred to stretch out the details, as we shall see, he would clearly be showing that he wanted to tell us many things other than the simple narrative of a deed done. It is therefore worthwhile to dig deeply into the details of the reading in order to bring to light the intentions of the evangelist.

Let us ask ourselves then who are the *persons* who are acting; what are the *signs* which John is putting in prominence; and what great *truths* are recalled.

The text says:

> On the third day there was a wedding feast at Cana in Galilee, and the mother of Jesus was there. Jesus and his disciples had likewise been invited to the celebration. At a certain point wine ran out, and Jesus' mother told him, "they have no more wine." Jesus replied, "woman, how does this concern of yours involve me? My hour has not yet come." His mother instructed those waiting on the table, "Do whatever he tells you." As prescribed for Jewish ceremonial washing, there were at hand six water jars, each holding fifteen to twenty-five gallons. "Fill those jars with water," Jesus ordered, at which they filled them to the brim. "Now," he said, "draw some out and take it to the waiter in charge." They did as he instructed them. The waiter in charge tasted the water made wine, without knowing where it had come from; only the waiters knew, since they had drawn the water. Then the waiter in charge called the groom over and

remarked to him: "People usually serve the choice wine first; then when the guests have been drinking awhile, a lesser vintage. What you have done is keep the choice wine until now." Jesus performed this first of his signs at Cana in Galilee. Thus did he reveal his glory, and his disciples believed in him. After this he went down to Capernaum, along with his mother and brothers (and his disciples) but they stayed there only a few days (John 2:1-12).

The persons

The mother of Jesus is the first person who is mentioned. Her name is not reported anywhere in the Gospel of John.

In our excerpt she is referred to a couple of times: "the mother" of Jesus is at the wedding feast; when wine is needed, the "mother" of Jesus indicates it to her son; then Jesus addresses her with the word "woman" and, notwithstanding his response, the "mother" tells the servers to do what he says.

At the end of the scene once again there is mention of the "mother" as she leaves with Jesus and the other disciples for Capernaum.

The story of Cana is first of all considered under the sign of the mother of Jesus, and the Pope makes full mention of it in his encyclical which was sent to the entire Church for the Marian Year.

Mary is addressed by Jesus as "woman" and that same title will come up again in the Gospel of John only at the moment of the cross, when Jesus presents her to the evangelist by saying to her: "Woman, there is your son" (John 19:26).

This shows that the event at Cana is read together with the incident at the cross, which tells us that the wedding feast is a veiled announcement of the mystery of redemption.

The second person in prominence is Jesus; he was invited to the wedding feast together with his disciples and, upon hearing his mother invite him to make some provision, replies to her first of all with a word which sounds like a refusal, but then gives the servant, twice, a command.

His presence is recalled toward the end of the incident: "Jesus performed this first of his signs at Cana in Galilee. Thus did he reveal his glory." This is a very important Chistological passage: here at Cana Jesus manifested his glory.

You will recall that, in the prologue, the evangelist John summarizes the entire mystery of the incarnation with the expression "We have seen his glory" (John 1:14). To emphasize, therefore, that Jesus manifested his glory at Cana suggests a tremendous mystery.

The third personage is represented by a category of persons, namely, the disciples: they were invited to the wedding, assisted in the event, and "believed" in Jesus. Evidently this is an extremely important moment even for the journey of the disciples.

The disciples are not the twelve apostles, as one might first think. At this point of the Gospel of John, there are only the first two disciples (John the Evangelist himself and Andrew) who followed the Lord at the invitation of John the Baptist, Simon whom Jesus had already met, Philip, and Nathanael.

Here are five men who timidly accompany Jesus and who initially do not understand very well what happened; afterwards they have a jolt and their eyes are opened to his glory.

The *servants* are also featured persons: they have the courage to believe the word of Mary, they have the courage to follow, without making too many problems, the commands of Jesus, and they are the ones who know what happened. They are among the very few who understand the deed.

The *waiter in charge* is another person in this episode. He is kind of a pitiful figure, because he did not keep track of the wine which was diminishing and then, realizing that he does not know how to explain the situation, makes up a funny truism as he calls the groom over.

This *headwaiter* did not understand that this was a manifestation of God. He represents a person involved in something larger than him/herself and who believes therefore that he is able to control the situation from the sideline.

The *groom* is the last person in the scene; he is also a figure very meagerly portrayed, apparently a person who remains in the background. The beneficiary of a great gift of divine power, he takes no notice of it.

A collection of very different persons: Mary, Jesus, the apostles, the servants, the head waiter, the groom, and naturally, the guests. Men and women, with their capabilities and incapabilities, their problems, their daily little schemes, form this scene. We can say that this is a small group gathered at a typical moment in everyday life—at a celebration, having fun at a banquet—in which Jesus intervenes with love and joy.

The symbols

This excerpt is also rich in its use of symbols: the indications of time and situations which in the light of the whole of Scripture takes on a meaning of the highest significance.

The marriage feast is that human reality in which one reads the mystery of Christ and the Church. As we know from Sacred Scripture, it is the symbol of the covenant, of the love of God for humanity.

"On the third day" is the expression which opens the account. In the New Testament this has a very precise meaning: the third day, in fact, is that of the resurrection. With this mysterious mention John reports to us a determined, precise theme: the resurrection of Jesus. The verse which immediately follows this event is interesting for it says; "As the Jewish Passover was near, Jesus went up to Jerusalem" (John 2:13). It is impossible to read the event we are studying except in the light of Easter.

And there's even more. The first chapter of John's Gospel is replete with chronological notes; "The next day" (John 1:29), John the Baptist saw Jesus approaching him; "The next day" (John 1:35), John the Baptist was there with two of his disciples; "The next day" (John 1:43) Jesus set out for Galilee. By adding all these days together, we notice that the evangelist has formed the structure of the first week of Jesus' ministry and in that structure the miracle of Cana is the climax. But the last week of the mystery of Jesus will also culminate in the definitive manifestation of the Lord, with new wine, with nuptial joy, with renewed humanity: it will, in a word, culminate in the resurrection.

In the marriage feast of Cana we have, as it were, the first symptom showing that Jesus came to renew the joy of humankind, a joy that had faded away because of difficulties and the daily struggles of life.

"My hour has not yet come" is another chronological reference rich in symbols.

Right from the beginning Jesus invites us to look to "his hour," that hour in which he, "realizing that the hour had come for him to pass from this world, rose from the meal, took off his cloak, picked up a towel, began to wash his disciples' feet" (John 13:1-5).

The miracle at Cana anticipates that final hour of the death of Jesus, of his resurrection, of his manifestation to humankind.

The wine is a very important symbolic element in Sacred Scripture. It is central to this event because first there is a diminishing supply, then the lack of wine is noticed, then there is a search to remedy the situation, and then, at last, there is plenty of wine.

The wine, and we shall meditate on that subject again tomorrow night, is a fundamental biblical image: "You put gladness into my heart more than when grain and wine abound," chants the psalmist (Ps 4:8). Wine is a symbol of the joy of God, of enthusiasm, of exuberant vitality. Wine finally is opposite to sadness, to daily routine, to repetitious activities, to tedium. It is the joyful exuberance of a person who lays aside precautions, fears, defense mechanisms, and reservations, and settles down.

It is the fundamental symbolic theme for understanding the significance of the story.

The six stone water jars are carefully described by John. Empty water jars, unable then to give what they were supposed to give; they should have contained oil or wine for the banquet, but in being empty they become a notable, cumbersome, and oppressive reality. They are a symbol of a dry, empty, uncertain, formal spirituality, of a spirituality which Jesus came to renew.

Finally, the water poured abundantly into the jars, capable of becoming a new reality, is a symbol of the richness and the bountifulness of the life of the Spirit, indicated precisely by the water which is poured out on the earth from an inexhaustible source.

As you see, there are so many signs and symbols in the Cana story that enrich other pages of Scripture and that make this narrative a mine rich in teachings for those who meditate on it with love, that it is really a condensation of divine mysteries.

The great truths

Especially in the last part of the story John the Evangelist explicitly emphasizes certain great truths:

"Jesus began his miracles";

"Jesus manifested his glory";

"The disciples believed in him."

As we have already recalled, the signs or miracles, glory, faith, and the Passover are truths of great theological meaning found in this passage.

I invite you, during the time for silence, to meditate on what has been said and to allow all the persons, situations, and symbols to begin to enter inside you. To meditate biblically, means to "chew again" on the text until we succeed in tasting it in all its profundity and then to feel that the Holy Spirit of God— who presents to us in Jesus the power of his historic action— is in us.

Conclusion

And so we have seen the different realities in the persons whom the evangelist has put before us. Humanity has been represented not only by the persons considered individually but also in those taken collectively, by groups (servants, disciples), and by the great institutions which are found among humans. We see both the natural institutions—marriage, celebration, banquet—and religious institutions—a religiousness which is dry, empty, inflexible, dull, incapable of satisfying persons, and then a new spirituality brought by Jesus which is the point of attention for Mary, a desire to benefit others, a capacity to fill the heart of humankind with joy.

"O Lord, grant that we may contemplate the richness of your revelation in these simple words of the evangelist. Permit us to be invited to the nuptials of your Word so that we can taste fully the wine of the spirit and be filled with the revelation, the richness of the Scriptures with which you want to nourish us all the days of this week. Permit us to penetrate some of the fundamental truths and decisive teachings of this gospel passage which is but a synthesis of your mystery of love, of redemption, of grace, of attention to humankind, of the offering of joy to your Church."

Try to consider, peacefully and serenely, the two questions I posed at the beginning:

Lord, what makes my joy fall short? What makes our joy fall short as a group, as a Church, as society?

Lord, what increase in joy do you wish to give us? What joy do you have in store for me to make me participate in this celebration, to take me from my difficulties and from my dryness, from my spirituality which is perhaps a bit lagging, tired out, weary, from the spirituality of our group which goes around in circles, as well as from our weariness with the Church?

"O Lord, I believe in you, I hope in you, I stake myself on you, because you, now that we have listened to the evangelical Word, want

to fill us with the new wine of your Spirit! And you, Mary, cause of our joy, help us to enter into this Word, and to prepare ourselves to meditate on the teachings and riches which the word contains for each of us!''

TWO

"They have no more wine"

"O Lord, we desire to dispose ourselves to listen to your Word, the inexhaustible source of life, to listen to Mary who said: They have no more wine! Mary, bring us to understand what you mean to suggest to us because we know that you pronounced those words in a very definite situation and yet you repeat them to us, for today's Church."

In his message for the World Youth Day, which will be celebrated next Sunday, Palm Sunday, John Paul II writes that Mary has expressed in the words uttered at Cana "the most profound secret of her life."

Therefore it is very important for us to know our Lady especially in view of her concerned statement: they have no more wine.

We have already seen how the excerpt from John on which we are meditating is a profound spring in which it is possible to distinguish three different levels. First of all the level of the event narrated: the persons, groups, situations, and symbols the evangelist presents to us in the historical reality of the occasion. Then there is the level of ecclesial prophecy: John and the early Church reflected on the text and accepted it as a prophecy about the Church. The third level is that of cosmic prophecy, in the sense that the episode is a prophecy about the world, about history as it is seen by God who saves.

Tonight we want to understand the meaning of the lack of wine at the level of our experience of Church and of society. The verse of the psalm; "You put gladness into my heart more than when grain and wine abound" (Ps 4:8), speaks of the joy of grain which is the joy of all the necessities for survival. We can think today of certain countries in the Third and Fourth World, especially of those countries subject to drought and other natural calamities: of Bangladesh, which I visited some weeks ago, and we can speak of the joy of "rice" which is the basic food of the area. When the season is good and they collect a certain amount of rice, the joy of the people is greatest because the fear of famine is removed for some months, until they have a flood or a deluge. For these people it means that Allah has assured them of a handful of rice every day, and there is an outbreak of joy.

But what can we understand by the joy of wine? There is still more joy here; not only the joy of survival, but the joy of celebration, of friendship, of the banquet, of the nuptials, of love, of new life, of victory.

The joy of wine is a sign of enthusiasm, of simplicity, of interior quiet; it is a symbol of the loosening of inhibitions, of fears which impede reciprocal communication. In the Bible, just as in the history of culture, wine is the symbol of a life which is unfolding, freely expanding, defining itself.

In the opposite sense, the lack of wine, in cultural and biblical symbolism, always means closing down, stiffening, creating suspicion, sadness, irritability, touchiness, argumentativeness, bad temper, pessimism, corrosive criticism, sourness.

A certain shame of the Gospel

In the Letter to the Romans (1:16), Saint Paul expresses these ideas: "I am not ashamed of the Gospel. It is the power of God." These are words that can be helpful in understanding the sad statement of Mary: they have no wine.

Let us then ask the Apostle: what reason do you have for being ashamed of the gospel? Why do you say: "I am not ashamed" instead of saying: "I am proud of the gospel, I give my life for the gospel"? What on earth is this shame of the gospel which you definitely put at a distance from you? Are you perhaps trying to make us understand by your denial that this shame could be in ourselves? What does it mean today to be ashamed of the gospel?

I believe that it must mean not only denying Jesus, as happened to Peter, but also agreeing to subtle forms of pride which are sometimes present in our contemporary existence even in the Church.

I think of three definite situations.

1. The first deals with the so-called dialogue. Paul VI, in his first encyclical entitled *Ecclesiam suam*, written in 1964, more than a year after he began his pontificate, and therefore after lengthy meditation, spoke in a magnificent way about dialogue, and introduced this theme into the Church, which the council took up at that point and made a classical theme.

We know what the conditions of dialogue are: that there be an esteem for the position of the other side, that something good in the positions of everyone is preserved, that the possibility not only to enrich others but to be enriched ourselves is retained.

Yet, what can come from the exercise of dialogue carried out under conditions that are not entirely correct? It can lead to a kind of uncertainty about one's own opinions, an inadequate assurance in oneself, because, if the other side is right, perhaps I am wrong. By involving myself in dialogue I can come to lose my own identity, to confuse it, to mix it up. In this way it can happen that I become ashamed of the gospel.

I recall in a press conference some weeks ago, held here in Milan for representatives of Christian Churches of Europe (Orthodox, Protestant, and Catholic), a journalist recalled one of his experiences in an ecumenical meeting. Among other things he said was that everybody was so kind, all searching for ways to say whatever was pleasing to the other persons who, in the long run, did not know any longer exactly what the particular positions were!

This is the risk of dialogue: at a certain point, without wishing it to be so, I find myself a bit ashamed of the gospel, of my profound conviction, and I try, even if only tactfully, to prescind from it.

2. The second situation has to do with the proper appreciation of other religions. In every religion there are some genuine values, and the council has vigorously affirmed this in its declaration *Nostra aetate* which takes up the subject of relationships with non-Christian religions. It is true that all religions can help people to search for God. However, another problem can arise from timidity of articulation. I have heard missionaries ask precisely this question: if people have these religious values, why do I ever have to disturb them? Would to God that I helped them to understand better, but with what right do I proclaim the gospel when they already have some of the means of salvation, although somewhat imperfectly?

Thus, agreeing with some of the important tenets of the council is joined to a kind of shame of the gospel.

3. The third situation, analogous with the preceding one, has to do with attention to the great human values.

Rightfully the constitution of the Second Vatican Council *Gaudium et spes* recognizes that it is possible for us everywhere to find some parts of Christian values, even in systems of thought which are very foreign to Christianity.

But in the desire to find them we risk compromising our faith and not knowing well enough what the gospel is trying to proclaim.

As a result there come sadness, uncertainty, timidity of the message, and confusion of ideas—these are really challenges to our contemporary conscience! As a result joy is missing: the wine of the gospel is missing because it is diluted, underdeveloped, set aside.

The challenge is such that it brings on the desire to give up on dialogue, not to accept the values of these other religions, to exorcise any human value except that of Christianity, for fear of losing that most precious treasure which is the joy of the gospel.

We cannot deny that in our time the lack of the wine of the gospel is felt; we do not even talk about evangelization and, what is more, there has never been so little courage to evangelize. Even in the missionary world, it is noted that there is an ennui with these discussions and questions: What then is missioning today, what sense is there in engaging in missionary work in our day?

You see how the words of Mary have acquired meaning: "They have no more wine," they lack the joy of the gospel. They have no more wine and they are waiting to drink. When at a meal something is lacking, someone suddenly gets up and runs to search for it on another table, or there is some irritation, nervousness, and discussion, and finally explicit notice is taken, so that everybody notices something missing! Then they begin to say: Whose fault is it? Who organized this celebration or this excursion, how come there was not enough for everyone? Why have we wasted what we had so that now there is not enough of it to serve us?

We see similar arguments in the story about the foolish and wise virgins. When the groom arrives it is asked who was so improvident as to cause the wine of the joy of the gospel to be lacking.

We make up certain theories, certain theologies which have created the situation of the lack of joy, of enthusiasm, of courage. We look for the culprit and we make up a sequence of events to explain the situation; we ask ourselves who had hidden the wine, who had squandered it, who carelessly dropped some of the bottles while carrying it from the wine cellar, who acted so clumsily.

The penetrating force of Mary's words, "the poorest have no more wine!" picture exactly our modern day situation.

Living the joy of the Gospel

"O Mary, you who had an abundance of joy with the family at Cana, give also to our family the wine of the gospel and, above all, make us understand in what this abundance of joy consists."

There are two little allegories which are most useful in this regard: "The reign of God is like a buried treasure which a man found in a field. He hid it again, and rejoicing at his find, went and sold all he had and bought that field. Or again, the kingdom of heaven is like a merchant's search for fine pearls. When he found one really valuable pearl, he went back and put up for sale all that he had and bought it" (Matt 13:44-46).

The joy of the gospel is like the joy of the one who, having found the treasure, becomes mad with joy, runs around in circles, sells everything, all his possessions, with the idea of buying the land which contains it. People look on him as mad, thinking that perhaps he has been blackmailed or has need of money because he has lost everything in a casino. But this man knows very well where he wants to go and it makes no difference to him what people say about him. The words and judgments of others do not affect him, because he knows that the treasure he found is worth more than all the rest.

The merchant who has found the pearl of great price sells everything and people think that he wants to change his job, that he is beside himself. But he knows that, when he has that most beautiful pearl, he has an asset greater than all the other pearls put together and, should he desire, he will also be able to buy everything else.

The joy of the gospel is characteristic of someone who, having found fullness of life, is unimpeded, free, noninvolved, not fearful, not entangled. Now, do you by any chance think that someone who found the precious pearl will despise all other pearls?

Absolutely not! Anyone who has found the precious pearl becomes capable of putting everything else in a proper scale of values, of comparing values, of judging them in relation to the most beautiful pearl. And this is done with extreme simplicity because, having the precious stone as a norm of comparison, one knows best the value of the others.

Whoever has found the treasure does not despise the rest, does not fear entering into negotiations with those who have the other treasures, because he or she is now in a position to give exact value to everything.

Let us hark back to the words of the gospel: "Whoever has will be given more, but the one who has not will lose the little he has" (Luke 19:26). To the one who has the joy of the gospel, to the one who has the precious pearl, the treasure, will also be given discernment of other values, of the values of other religions, of human values outside of Christianity; this person will be given the capacity to dialogue without fear, without sadness, without reticence, even with joy, which is proper because he or she will recognize the values of every other thing. To the one who has the joy of the gospel will be given an intuitive sense of the truth which can exist in other religions.

On the other hand, from those who do not have will be taken also that which they have. To those who possess only slight joy of the gospel, the ability to dialogue will be squelched and they will be hardened in the defence of that little which they do possess, they will become closed in on themselves, they will be put in opposition with others for fear of losing what little they have. This is our picture, the picture of our society. Our little joy of the gospel is the reason for the shabbiness, for the sadness in every area of ecclesiastical and social life, for the narrowness of heart, and is the cause for arguments over little things.

It is our Lady who tells us: If you do not have the joy of the gospel, you will perish in your sadness.

"O Mary, you who have made a diagnosis of our society, and of that which sometimes afflicts us as Christians, while sadly advising your son: 'They have no more wine!,' grant us to open our hearts to the true joy of the gospel. Grant us, O Mother, to understand what is really valuable, because the joy of the gospel is, exactly, of the

gospel, *not simply any joy, but that which comes from the unlimited welcome given to the divine initiative of love for me, in the crucified Jesus."*

Anyone who searches for joy in human assurances, in ideologies, in trifles, cannot find this joy. The joy of the gospel is Jesus crucified who fills our life by forgiving our sins, by giving us the sign of his infinite love, by filling each of our days and nights with his profound joy.

The joy of Cana is Mary who comes into our hearts with her tenderness, goodness, compassion, and mercy.

When we lack freedom, when we are frightened, lazy, timid, worried about the future of the Church and our community, this does not mean that we have lost the joy of the gospel but only some shadow, some distant, intellectual abstract of the gospel. The reason, as St. Paul emphasizes, is that the gospel is not doctrine, theory, but the power of God for salvation for anyone who believes. To welcome the gospel is to welcome its power.

Mary, therefore, invites us to welcome the power of the gospel, to consider joy, to rivet our eyes on it; she invites us to entrust ourselves to Christ crucified who desires to fill us with his joy.

Questions for meditation

In conclusion I would like to propose certain practical reflections for the period of silence which, as I have said, is the pearl of all our activity. Even if we find it tiresome, I am sure that we will experience a great benefit for our life. Let us prepare ourselves for it with the following questions:

Do I have the joy of the gospel in me? Have I ever experienced such joy? What is it and how is it manifested in me? How is it that there is one joy which surpasses all others and which does not deny the others but ratifies, includes, welcomes, judges, and realigns them?

Grant me, O Lord, the joy of the gospel because there is no treasure more precious than it, there is none which can be compared with it and makes the pain of selling everything else to buy it worthwhile.

What steps do I feel I have to take to open myself up to the joy of the gospel, to consent to that little or that much which is already in me?

Indeed the joy of the gospel is not only like a pearl; it is true that Jesus compares it to a pearl but he also compares it to flowing water and therefore it is not something that can be kept in a refrigerator! The joy of the gospel either acts or it wastes away; either it breaks out into a bud or it rots. Frequently it is given to us, but we do not accept it at once, we do not complete the little steps which are suggested to us, and so they flee from our heart.

What step do I want to take, O Lord, to give space to this joy?

The first step we are taking right here in these exercises is the sacrifice, the will, and the perseverance with which we follow them. We give you, O Lord, all this with joy. Thank you, Lord, for you have called us to this act.

We then think in our hearts about what other step we should take to carry this out and we think to ourselves of taking it now, immediately, not tomorrow. The movements are made above all in the heart, and if we make this decision this evening, our joy begins to flourish.

Let me make a suggestion. Each of you experiences within yourself situations of discomfort—at home, in school, at work, with companions, with persons who ought to be friends to us. It is a situation which burdens us, a person whom we do not accept, a fact which disgusts us. Let us come face to face with this situation saying, "Lord, I thank you because in these irksome, uncomfortable, and difficult situations you give me a providential occasion to live the gospel with friendship, forgiveness, sacrifice, renunciation, and peace."

If we take this step, if we make the decision to pray in this way, we light a fuse for the joy of the gospel, the joy of the Crucified one who comes into our life.

"O Mary, open our hearts because we are deaf to your words: they have no more wine! Open our hearts so that we deservedly allow ourselves to be reproached by you and we can then obtain that gift of reconciliation and joy which Jesus prepares for us."

THREE

"Thus did he reveal his glory"

Let us contemplate this evening the mystery of the Cross beginning with the words which are found toward the end of the story of Cana: "Thus did Jesus reveal his glory, and his disciples believed in him" (John 2:11).

Mary, you who stood close to the cross of the Lord, grant us to know the heart of this mystery and to understand how Jesus revealed his glory by the miracle of water changed into wine.

In fact, by reading the narrative we note at first glance a certain disproportion between that small domestic deed, known only to a few people, and the interpretation of the evangelist who says, "He revealed his glory."

The joy of the Cross

Last evening we tried to explain the words of Mary: "They have no more wine." Our Lady, we are told there, gives this warning indicating to us that the wine is the joy of the gospel, and that too often we lack it. It is lacking in many baptized persons who live out their days by literally dragging themselves along, by plodding along under the troubles of life, with more afflictions than satisfactions.

Joy is missing in the ordinary ecclesiastical administration of worship and in pastoral ministry, and our gatherings, our communities, sometimes show the poverty of joy. It is missing among many groups and congregations, as one of you wrote to me after last evening's reflection: "The joy of the gospel is lacking among us Christians of the West in so many ways: people fed up, worn-out and disillusioned, mad with sex, missing the joy of the just. This leads to an increase in suspicion or a search for palm readers, and words and meetings are multiplied while there is a drop in fervor and duty."

Our Lady knows all this and she is close to us.

However, from a discussion which I had today, I have begun to think that perhaps not all those who followed the meditation—especially those who followed by radio outside the atmosphere of prayer in which we are living—have rightly understood what the joy of the gospel signifies. It is not the joy found just in the mere reading of the words of Scripture, even if by reading them we are able to experience a certain joy.

The joy of the gospel, which Paul defines as "the power of God leading everyone who believes in it" (Rom 1:16), is the joy of knowing that God is communicating with me. Why do you, O my God, love me in spite of everything, why do you love this humanity of ours, why did you redeem it, why have you loved us by giving us your Son, why have you not abandoned us, why are you Father to me and why do you communicate with me by an uninterrupted cascade of graces?

The joy of the gospel is the joy coming from the good news that God loves us sinners, desperate, scattered, bewildered, and leads us back to his great intimacy. And this joy of the gospel has its culmination mysteriously in the cross.

It is not by accident that this evening we are contemplating the cross while looking at the same time at the relics before which Saint Charles Borromeo and others of our fathers in the faith have prayed.

The good news that God communicated to me with ineffable and merciful love has its culmination in the cross.

Naturally we can spend many years, as we make our pilgrim way, before really understanding the relationship between the gospel and the cross, even if it is proclaimed from the very beginning of our life of faith. The Apostle Paul began his preaching by solemnly declaring the cross and yet several years of experience, of disillusions, were necessary for him before reaching the actual intuition of its centrality.

For us too many years of Christian life can pass by, even of priestly and religious life, before really being illumined on the centrality of the mystery of the cross, on the identity between the cross and glory.

While meditating on the words of John, "He revealed his glory," let us ask Mary to dispose us for this gift.

The glory of God

The statement of the evangelist, as I said, startles us because it seems disproportionate to the modesty of the event which, among others, the Synoptics did not record, leaving us to suppose that they had very little memory of its tradition.

But we are all the more startled by noticing, if we continue reading the Fourth Gospel, that in chapter 7 John notes, "Jesus had not yet been glorified" (John 7:39). Only from chapter 12 onward does he begin to speak of the glorification of Jesus: "The hour has come for the Son of Man to be glorified," says the Lord (John 12:23); and after the washing of feet, when the betrayal of Judas is announced and Judas departs to carry out his crime, Jesus exclaims, "Now is the Son of Man glorified" (John 13:31). In his final prayer during the Last Supper, he says: "Father, give glory to your son" (John 17:1).

This glory of Jesus is finally manifested at the end of his life: in the betrayal, in his death, in the cross. Even the prologue of the Gospel of John implies this: "The Word became flesh and made his dwelling among us"—let us look for this glory, even here in the midst of our poor camp tents, so that it becomes accessible to us—"and we have seen his glory, the glory of an only son coming from the Father, filled with enduring love" (John 1:14).

John saw this glory at the moment when Jesus, nailed to the cross after having been given vinegar to drink, said, "Now it is finished"; and again at the moment when one of the soldiers struck his heart with a lance and from it came forth blood and water (John 19:30-37).

We can understand the manifestation of the glory of Jesus at Cana only by beginning with contemplation of the pierced, crucified Savior, with contemplation on his sorrowful death on the cross.

The glory of which Scripture speaks repeatedly is the splendor of God, the overflowing of his power, the richness, goodness, and tenderness of God who intervenes in history. This is glory: the divine splendor which intervenes in history and is made visible.

In the Old Testament, the divine glory is perceived by humankind in magnificent manifestations of nature; we think of thunder, lightning, storms, earthquakes, and the fire at Sinai.

How is it possible that the overflowing power of God is completely concentrated in Jesus and in his cross? How is it possible to state that in his cross we see his glory? By what sign is his death manifested as glory? Why do we call glory the flow of blood and water from the side of Jesus, after the last blow inflicted on his tormented body? Isn't this rather an ignominy, a cruelty, an injustice or, at best, the silence of God in history?

We will understand the mystery of the glory of the Lord by starting with the story of Cana and rereading the entire Gospel as a follow-up, looking for little signs of the great glory of God on Calvary.

The manifestation of the glory at Cana

At Cana Jesus voluntarily multiplied the wine for the joy of people. A little later he cured the paralytic, multiplied the loaves, restored health to a sick person, gave sight to the man born blind, and raised Lazarus from the dead.

The glory of God, finally, is the fact that we live, that we do not die, that we enjoy, that we do not suffer sadness. *The glory of God is our joy.* God is the one who expends himself completely for our joy, he is the one who gives his complete self to rescue us from our sadness, who takes on himself our sorrows, who burdens himself with them to the utmost, who does not put limits on the manifestation of his love for us, for each one of us.

This is how we can have an intimation of the mystery of glory if we contemplate Jesus who died on the cross. The culminating moment of the glory of God, the moment at which his glory is revealed in a radiant way, indisputably, is when Jesus voluntarily accepts death because of his *love of humankind* communicating the Spirit, saving us from sin, restoring peace and life to us. Henceforth we can no longer doubt that God loves us to the very end. The cross is the supreme sign of the tenderness of God and therefore of his glory.

"Grant us, O Lord, the grace to understand that precisely in the cross, in the crucifixion, in the humiliation, is manifested your glory of love freely given to humankind, is manifested your most intimate nature. Indeed you are the one who has given without limits and your giving of yourself does not appear in the thunder, in the wind, in the storms, in victory over your enemies. It was evident, to some extent, in the cure of sickness, it appears in the wine at Cana and in the paralytic who got up and walked. But above all it appears when you, O Lord, gave everything to the utmost, when you had nothing more than you had already given for me.

"This is your glory, even if we do not succeed in expressing it with adequate words."

The glory of God is manifested in all the activities of Jesus as the giver of life and yet it finds its greatest expression in the cross.

Cana is the first announcement of it: there we see the concern of our Lord for humankind, his tenderness, his kind ac-

ceptance of Mary's invitation, even if the hour of the cross had
not yet arrived.

Cana is the manifestation of glory because it is God's love
for humankind.

The glory of God is shown in great things; not however
by things shining brightly in the eyes of the world, but by proof
of a surplus of love and kindness. This surplus, so extraordinary, incredible, and unsurpassable, of love and kindness is
found in the Lord's knowing how to lose everything for us,
in his knowing how to forgive everything, at the moment of
the death on the cross of his Son.

The glory of God is indeed manifested in the little things,
in ordinary deeds, at Cana. And it is the same glory which appeared on the cross, which was lived each moment of the day
in gratuitous surrender.

Every little gesture of ours showing gratitude, therefore,
shows the glory of the Lord. And just as you, O Jesus, by
manifesting at Cana your glory brought the disciples to believe
in you, so now may we become credible every time that with
joy we show your glory in acts of gratuitous and authentic self-
denial.

In our manner of praying this evening, in our manner of
meeting people, of handshaking, in our manner of taking in-
terest in others, of giving them our attention, of not passing
by with disinterest the needs of our brothers and sisters, we
show the glory of God.

Little by little we will become capable of manifesting it in
particular trials, in important moments of our lives, because
even in the beginning, in little things of everyday life, we
listened, as did Jesus, to the prompting of Mary.

The path to peace

By way of coming to a close I would like to draw a final
conclusion from the meditation on Jesus who at Cana
manifested his glory. This glory in our day is manifested in
a particular manner, in this efficiency-driven society of ours,
with a homily on peace.

The recognition of the glory of Jesus on the cross, when it is received into human hearts, produces a practice of active and generous nonviolence, which brings the victory of the cross into the world. The Christian non-violence of the gospel is a transferral of the glory of the cross to the high efficiency and fearful stress in our society.

Lord, you have called us to bring ourselves to learn from the glory of the cross, through the little gestures at Cana, how to reeducate our society, sick as it is with tensions, aggressiveness, and war, by means of the cleansing and purification which the deeds of peace, nonviolence, produce in everyday life.

Every renunciation of aggressiveness, vindictiveness, irritating touchiness, or vain spitefulness is a weeding out of aggression, a victory of the cross of Jesus, a serious and progressive education of humanity in the glory of peace.

"O Mary, queen of peace, purify our hearts of all those acts of aggression, which make our hearts grow dim, and grant us also to fill each of our days with deeds of forgiveness."

And in the moments of silence, which will be at the same time moments of adoration of the cross, let us pray in these words:

"O Lord, make us understand the mystery of your joy, of your glory, and of your cross. Bring me to see how much aggressiveness, resistance to others, distrust, and fear there is in me. Free me, O Lord, and make clear to me everything in me that is in opposition to others. Make me walk the path of your peace."

FOUR

"Do whatever he tells you"

I received a letter from a young lady who is participating in these exercises in which she described a comparison between the experiences of prayer and the sports in which she engages. The note is very pleasant one and I quote certain parts from it because they encourage us to acquit ourselves well on our pilgrimage.

> The beginning of athletics. Someone told me that I could engage in sports. I was not skillful, but sports could be a help to me in the future. Someone told me that prayer was a wonderful experience which would help me to grow.
> The first steps. When I began sports I was stubborn, the body did not always respond to the demands which I made, it seemed that I got nothing out of them except some muscle pain. Prayer. When I began I was stubborn, it was tiresome to pray. I made my body physically tired by standing still so I could be concentrated, keep silent, recall my thoughts about God. It seemed like time lost, it seemed that I was accomplishing nothing.
> After some time. After some time in training, the body began to react, you get less tired, you succeed better in putting yourself in motion, in resisting tiredness. The demands for a time seemed then easy. And yet you can increase your work load a bit. Prayer. After some time it no longer bothers you to stand still, for the time to search into yourself, to dialogue with

God. Then you think that someone is talking to you, you manage to stand longer, the time goes by quickly, that time which you always thought to be slow.

I will stop with that, while hoping that at the end of our exercise, the time will begin to go quickly, even the minutes of silence, and that in any case each one of you will have the determination to persevere in the exercise of the spirit, just as we have the determination and the desire to persevere in the exercise of the body even if it causes some fatigue.

We want now to reflect on those words of Mary which formed the title of the message of the Pope for the World Youth Day: "Do whatever he tells you" (John 2:5).

Last evening I tried to show that the glory of Jesus, manifested at Cana, is the same as what showed forth on the cross, and that from it are derived definite consequences about the meaning of life and the little things of every day, about the manner of conducting ourselves in society. I would have liked to pause a little longer on the wine of our joy, which is poured out into our hearts from the love of Jesus crucified for humankind, the love that shines forth resplendently on the cross. Paradoxically the joy of humankind comes from the cross of Jesus and, in contemplating the Crucified One, there is offered to us the joy of the gospel, the joy of feeling ourselves loved by God.

I noticed that I did not succeed in expressing the multitude of thoughts which were prompting me from within; therefore this evening we take up once again the theme from another point of view, precisely the theme of the very simple words addressed by our Lady to the servants of the banquet at Cana.

The words of Mary—where did they come from?

The Pope writes, "Do whatever he tells you." By these words Mary has expressed above all *the profound secret of her own life*. Behind these words she fully stands (Message for the Third World Youth Day, no. 2).

In what sense, O Mary, have you expressed the most profound secret of your life in this invitation to the servants at Cana?

From what profound experience do these words come forth from you? A phrase similar to yours in the Book of Genesis comes to mind, when the Egyptians, finding themselves without food because of the great famine, are told by the Pharaoh, "Go to Joseph; do whatever he tells you" (Gen 41:55). These are words which already have a history of providence in particularly difficult and hard times.

In Mary, the words came first of all from a personal trial. This is not just a moment of enthusiasm, of euphoria, but rather a moment of pain, even if it is covered up.

And so Mary, while she expresses the invitation with calmness, hides a suffering analogous to the suffering of the Syro-Phoenician woman about whom we read in the Gospel according to Matthew. Jesus travelled to the area of Tyre and Sidon; the woman, a native of those regions, requested Jesus to cure her son. The Lord, after the disciples pleaded with him to listen to the lady, replied, "My mission is only to the lost sheep of the house of Israel." At this point the poor woman said to him, "Even the dogs eat the leavings that fall from their masters' tables" (Matt 15:21-28). Certainly the woman had experienced a feeling of hardship, of suffering; she felt rejected. But notwithstanding that, she had a tremendous confidence in Jesus. So too the centurion had gone to him to beseech him to cure his seriously ill son and Jesus replied with one expression which we can read as a question: "Perhaps I ought to come to your house?" In doing so he noted that a Jew did not enter the house of a pagan. But the man had the courage to say: "I am not worthy to have you under my roof. Just give an order and my boy will get better" (Matt 8:5-13).

There is another situation which reminds us of Mary. The episode has to do with the royal official; Jesus had gone once again to Cana of Galilee and the servant, who had a son ill, implored him to come to his house to cure him. Jesus said to him, "Unless you people see signs and wonders, you do not believe." The man, feeling aggrieved, insisted, "Sir, come down before my child dies" (John 4:46-54).

Now, Mary had heard this response from her son: "Woman, how does this concern of yours involve me? My hour has not yet come" (John 2:4). Exegetes interpret these words of Jesus in different ways, but they are certainly not an enthusiastic acceptance of the mother's proposal and she would have been able to pull back. Often we, in similar situations, get irritated and decide to wash our hands of the whole thing, to let things go as they were supposed to go. Mary however knows that this was a test: the test of faith.

She does not get annoyed, she does not take offence, but perseveres and says to Jesus: No matter what it seems like on the outside I entrust everything to you with full confidence, my Son, and I invite the others to obey you without hesitation.

These words of hers express indeed the overcoming of a trial, of the silence of God.

In the encyclical *Redemptoris Mater,* the Pope noted several times that our Lady was tested in her faith.

In the second place, the invitation to the servants comes from a profound inclination of heart on the part of Mary. Her words repeat the primordial yes of the annunciation. "Behind all these words there She stands. Her life has in fact been one grand yes to our Lord, a yes full of joy and confidence. Mary, full of grace, Immaculate Virgin, has lived her entire life in a total openness to God and that even in the most difficult moments that reached their climax on the peak of Mount Calvary, at the foot of the cross. She never retracted her yes" (Message of the Pope for the Third World Youth Day, no. 2).

Here at Cana Mary's yes can be interpreted with the words: You also be prepared to do what he asks you to do, everything that God tells you, because human beings find their true well-being in doing the will of God.

Our Lady does indeed not know what Jesus might say to the servants, she does not know if he will work a miracle or if he will send them to buy some wine; she knows nothing. In the Greek text, in fact, the words sound much like some indefinite expression: *"whatever he has to tell you, that do."* God does not abandon his children who are in need, even if the need is very small.

In the heart of Mary who pronounces these words there is certitude that it is necessary to put trust in God, there is great hope that does not fade because Jesus is the way out of apparently closed situations.

The invitation of Mary to the servants also sprang from her hope.

Finally, the words "Do whatever he tells you" come from a very practical spirit. Mary does not ask the servants to give careful consideration to the problem, nor does she search into the causes or try to find out who was to blame for the lack of wine; she simply says: Do it, get to work.

She knows that not the one who says, "Lord, Lord," but rather those who do the will of God will enter into the kingdom of heaven; whoever hears the words and puts them into practice is like the wise man who built his house on rock (Matt 7:21-27).

Mary knows very well that they are "blessed who hear the word of God and keep it" (Luke 11:28), not those who study it and who discuss it around the table. "Do whatever he tells you."

The words of Mary summon us

Now I propose to take up again the four profound motives that gave birth to the words of our Lady, by way of meditation (the second step of the *lectio divina*), by putting ourselves in Mary's place and there questioning ourselves.

Are we living these attitudes? In her situation would we have expressed ourselves as she did?

1. The test of the silence of God. First of all, we ask ourselves if we can pass the test of an apparent refusal by Jesus.

Do we sometimes live moments in which we experience the silence of God, moments in which it seems he does not respond to us or responds to us by doing the opposite of what we have asked of him? What is stirred up in us in the face of such situations?

Sadness is born, distrust in God. Not only on a personal level, but also on the level of society: bitterness, injustices, cruelties in the social situation of humanity—I think, for example, of those described in the Pope's encyclical *Sollicitudo rei socialis*—bring many people to conclude that God surely has abandoned the world.

This trial of the silence of God wears down the modern spirit, makes it suspicious: does God really want our well-being?

There is question here of a very subtle temptation on the part of contemporary humans who do not know how to recognize the test of faith, who are entrenched in God's silence and think it final.

How different the soul of Mary who overcame the test immediately, knowing that God does not deceive, that he has a heart bigger than hers.

How different is the biblical soul which is expressed, for example, in the Book of Lamentations of Jeremiah, which I reread these past few days because it seems rich in indications regarding some of the great sufferings of the Church and of society. Lamentations contains very strong phrases, which sound at first like curses and recall the protests of Job: "He has broken my teeth with gravel, pressed my face in the dust. I have forgotten what happiness is; I tell myself my future is lost, all that I hoped for from the Lord" (Lam 3:16-18).

Humankind is bewildered in the presence of the silence of God as we chant in Psalm 66: "You have tested us, O God! You have tried us as silver is tried by fire. You have brought us into a snare; you laid a heavy burden on our backs. You let men ride over our heads; but you have led us out to refreshment" (vv. 10-12).

But the Book of Lamentations continues: "But I will call this [these tests, humiliations, this retreat] as my reason to have hope: the favors of the Lord are not spent; they are renewed each morning, so great is his faithfulness. . . . Good is the Lord to one who waits for him, to the soul that seeks him. It is good to hope in silence for the saving help of the Lord" (Lam 3:21-31, 25-26).

Let us ask ourselves: Is my reaction to the test, to the silence of God, to heaven closed down to me, the same as Mary's reaction, the same as that of the biblical person?

2. The attitude of the human heart. We have said that the words "Do whatever he tells you" came from a profound inclination in Mary's heart to do what God wanted, with the conviction that this is the good of a person.

In reality, contemporary humans, just like humans of all times when stuck in their own worldliness, have a spontaneous attitude of opposition: I know what is best for me, my enjoyment, my advantage, my time is my own, my stomach is mine. My well-being is not that which God wants for me.

Human beings believe in their absolute power to buy their well-being: I pay you and you are mine!

The yes of Mary is quite a revolutionary program: "Be it done unto me according to your Word," your good is my good, my good is yours. She "responded with all her human 'I,' in true womanly fashion, and in such a response of faith there was both a perfect cooperation with the grace of God which came and gave help and also a perfect availability to the action of the Holy Spirit" (*Redemptoris Mater*, no. 13, cited in the Message for the Third World Youth Day).

Let us try during the moment of silence that we will have shortly to agree among ourselves with the words of Mary saying, "Lord, you are the guide of my life."

And let us ask ourselves: What do these words excite in me? Perhaps they cause fear in me, because I do not find myself ultimately trusting fundamentally in the Lord.

But fear is natural, because I can say these words only through grace, through a gift of God. It is his gift for me to entrust myself to him and in this only to find myself again. Indeed the expression "You, O Lord, are the guide of my life, do with me according to your will" represents the conviction that the good is willed by God, that God cannot will it, if it is not my good.

In what, on the other hand, does original sin consist? In doubt that perhaps God does not desire our good, that perhaps what he commands for us is something which is not useful for us.

"You are the guide of my life" is exactly the contrary of doubt, and it is the word of Jesus on the cross. He receives on his shoulders the tree of the cross to fulfill the mandate of God, embracing to the absolute fullest the project of the Father, which is to will everything good for every human and to rescue every person from every evil, to love humanity without ever looking back. I could, says Jesus, call twelve legions of angels, but then I would not be faithful to the mandate of my Father.

Jesus therefore identifies his good with the will of the Father and identifies my good with his; he is identified with my good through love. It is a wonderful process of loving identification, of *transferrence* as we might call it, by which my good is his and to die for me is his good, because it is identified with my good, in such a way that I might know how to be identified with his will, with that which he thinks good for me.

The words of Mary, "Do whatever he tells you" (you are my project) touch the fundamental concept of life, understand life as a gift, a task, entrusted to one. Mary has a substantial confidence in life throughout every moment, including the most dramatic, or most obscure.

Even when we might be struck with a critical illness, even then we can say, "You are the guide of my life." This is so because Jesus, faced with condemnation to death, has spoken these words to the Father *for me*, and he died to be identified with my good.

What formidable consequences these words have! O Jesus, bring them close to our lives, because our life changes when we feel ourselves so identified with you, by your gift on the cross.

3. Our anxieties. In the heart of Mary there is a third attitude: the great hope that God never disappoints. "Do whatever he tells you" indicates the certainty that God will surely say something, that God never leaves us without a way out.

In reality, we often despair of finding a way out; two or three problems are enough to disturb us, to make us feel trapped. The perception of having made a mistake and of coming into a situation with no way out is one of the most bitter in life. Perhaps I have made a mistake about my choice of life, about certain things I have done which have complicated my life and I feel blackmailed by others: in every case, I think that I have no way of getting out.

The words of Mary express the opposite: Do what he tells you because the way out is there. There is a way out for every one of our quandries, for the world which seems to us to be condemned to war, to hunger, to ecological disaster.

From such certainty arise the energies for renewal. This is the reason the great assembly of all Christians of Europe—Orthodox, Protestant, Catholics—which we are now preparing for in 1990 and for which we are taking the theme "Peace, justice, safeguarding of creation" will be a formidable proclamation of the fact that in the will of God there can come an end to atomic, nuclear, and military danger, as well as to hunger and underdevelopment.

The most recent letter of John Paul II on the occasion of the millennium of the baptism of Russia is full of this hope: there is a way out of the divisions among the Churches and the great East-West blocs. Our Lady, whom we celebrate in this millennium of the baptism of Russia, has for us the way out.

4. The conversational spirit. We have said, finally, that the invitation of Mary to the servants stresses a practical spirit.

Her words are oriented to the practical: "do" (not: think, daydream, reflect), and are in contrast to an excessive theoretical and talkative spirit which we find at times in the Church. That is the spirit of those who believe that problems are not sufficiently clarified, that it is necessary to get to the bottom of a problem before acting, to reexamine it, to plan around a table, to hold meetings.

Evidently what is important is reflection, meditation as contemplative attitude, but if the "doing" is constantly postponed it becomes an alibi.

The true Marian contemplative spirit is the spirit that, through an effective and practical contemplation, tends toward compassion, tenderness, the immediate actions of the good Samaritan, and what Mary did at Cana, which we are contemplating in these exercises.

"Mary, grant that we may participate in your practical compassion, the fruit of contemplative spirit, just as you wished to participate with all your strength in your trial, in your obedience to the will of God, in your trust in the Lord and his life. Grant that we may adore your Son in the Eucharist, that we may be able to listen to his words and to do whatever he tells us."

FIVE

Mary as missionary

"Hail, through You glory shines forth;
Hail, through You sorrow is wiped out . . .
Hail, guide to celestial wisdom;
Hail, proof of enigmatic mystery."

These words and others from the marvelous Byzantine
hymn *Akathistos,* which we have sung, will accompany us in
the celebration of the feast of the Annunciation, the prime feast
of our Lady, the beginning of all the liturgical solemnities in
her honor; it is the one which recalls for us the Marian year
which the Pope desired to inaugurate a year ago; it is the one,
lastly, which concludes our exercises during which we have
prayed together as we meditated on the mystery of Mary and
of Jesus at the wedding feast of Cana.

The journey covered

Before reflecting on the missionary role that Mary taught
to the Church in the mystery of Cana, I would like briefly to
review what we have learned up to this point.

The choice of a selection from John's Gospel has certainly
been a bit bold. The Fourth Gospel is really the book for the
mature Christian, for the contemplative Christian; it presup-
poses a practical knowledge and a walk taken in accordance
with the stages of the other Gospels—of Mark, Matthew, and

Luke. In John everything is contemplated as a unit and every episode, in some way or the other, recalls all the other gospel events; it recalls the mystery of God, that is the Father who reveals the Son, the Son who gives his life on the cross, and the Church who is born from the cross of Jesus, saved humanity.

And this is why to meditate on the event at Cana we must refer to the prologue, to the passion, to the pierced side of Jesus, to Mary who is near the cross of her son who dies out of love.

The Gospel of John offers us a contemplative and global look. I tried to stress this on the first evening by presenting the overall scene with its multiplicity of persons, signs, symbols, and the realities they evoke, so that we might dispose ourselves with minds and hearts open to the riches of revelation expressed in these few lines. If John had not handed down the episode of Cana, we would have been deprived of one of the most beautiful passages of Scripture.

On the second evening we concentrated on the particular but central symbol of the excerpt, the wine: the wine that is lacking, the wine whose lack Mary notices, the wine that abounds.

We asked ourselves what is the symbolic significance of the wine incident selected by John and we replied that it is the joy of the gospel.

We were also able to reply: it is the faith, it is the grace of the New Testament. All this is signified by the wine.

In our desire to understand better why the symbol of wine was chosen, wine which in itself does not represent an absolute necessity and is only a spark, a burst, a sparkle that gives enthusiasm, we said that the question here is not about pure faith, about faith necessary for our salvation. The wine is not a pure grace that prevents us from dying in the state of serious sin, from going to hell. Rather, it is the joy of faith, the enthusiasm of faith, its cheerfulness, the Christian life in so far as it is joy and cheerfulness.

And so it becomes clear that wine is lacking for the Church today: it lacks the joy of the gospel. There are certainly some seeds of Christian life, some attempts at communitarian life, but there is no breath, no enthusiasm. Thus we fixed our attention on the most precious gift, the pearl, on that treasure which is the joy of the gospel.

On the third evening we asked where it comes from, since such joy is not bought in the marketplace, nor found by reading books or attending a summer course of studies, nor even by participating in a course of exercises.

I recall, by the way, a very beautiful quotation from Pascal which states: "I acknowledge, O my God, that my heart is so hardened, so full of ideas, concerns, disturbances, and attachments to the world, that neither sickness, nor health, nor discourses, nor books, nor your Sacred Scriptures, nor your gospel, nor your most sacred mysteries, nor miracles, not the use of the sacraments, not the sacrifice of your body, not all my own strength, nor that of the entire world, none of these can bring about my conversion if you do not accompany all these things with the extraordinary assistance of your grace" (B. Pascal, *The Good Use of Illnesses*, Prayer 4, [Vicenza: La Locusta, 1986]).

In our meditation we understood that the joy of the gospel comes from the glory of God which overflows down to us, and does not come from the reading of the gospels or from spending a long time on our knees or from any of our own resources.

The origin of the joy of the gospel is God himself in so far as he is communicated, manifested as love, life, vitality; it is his glory. It is the glory that Jesus manifests in the mystery of Cana, it is the power of God communicated to humankind. We can also say that the source of our joy is the Holy Spirit who is the glory of God radiated upon humanity.

If joy is missing for us it is useless to search for it in books or on the streets. We must open our heart to the fullness of the gift of God which attracts us to him, unites us to the glory of Christ, makes of us a single bond with Jesus who communicates to us the Spirit in superabundance.

How by this means is the Spirit, the glory of God, the joy of the gospel communicated to us? Not by a simple mystical contact with the deity, nor by any kind of compenetration of the mystery of God with the poverty of our life; it occurs only by way of the cross. The cross is the precise and concrete way through which God gives us the joy of the gospel. It is in this way the glory of God is manifested and bursts forth in history by the death of Jesus on the cross. Through the cross it is communicated to us as a gift, as life, just as the blood and water which poured forth from the side of Jesus crucified irrigated the world.

The wine of the joy of the gospel comes necessarily and only by means of the love of the Crucified one who has loved us to the end and has risen for us. It is here finally that we can obtain it. When we say that Jesus resolves all our problems, that he is our life, we must always understand Jesus crucified and risen. In these words, "I am the way, and the truth, and the life; no one comes to the Father but through me" (John 14:6), Jesus refers to himself as the one who died for us, who saved us by the cross, who in this incredible mystery of weakness, poverty, and ignominy shows the power, grace, and infinite mercy of the Father. Behold the glory of the cross from which the Church receives the glory of the gospel.

On the fourth evening we asked how this glory of the cross works in us in a concrete way and we understood from the words of Mary, "Do whatever he tells you," that it works through obedience to Jesus, through acceptance of God's goal for us.

When I succeed in saying to Jesus crucified, risen, and glorified, "You are the guide of my life," then the glory of the cross enters into us and joy transforms us, vivifies our communities, our Church, humanity.

After having tried to contemplate little by little the wonderful fresco of the redemption which was the mysterious event at Cana it remains for us now to try to understand in what way the glory of the cross—which through the acceptance of the goal of the crucified Lord risen for us becomes the joy of the gospel, the joy of our heart—is spread. In what way, therefore, does the Church become missionary?

This is a question which young people often pose to me when I meet them in parishes: how is it possible for our group to become missionary? Then, strange as it may seem, the young people add: We feel a bit left out, we feel like we are running around in circles, that we are prisoners of our own problems, and for this reason we would like to be more missionary, more expansive.

We put this question before our Lady: How are you, O Mary, a missionary of the joy of Christ crucified, of the glory, of the gift of the Holy Spirit which gives joy to the heart of humankind?

Our Lady gives us in the scene of Cana the model of a missionary Church, of a Church fully aware of the lack of faith and of joy that afflicts such a great part of humanity.

The prime source of the missionary Church

"At a certain point the wine ran out, and Jesus' mother told him, 'They have no more wine' " (John 2:3). I would like to point out to you that the gospel account is really strange and improbable.

We could put together a probable scenario of the events in the following way: during a banquet the wine runs out; the servants notice it; concerned, they advise the head waiter. These same servants suddenly leave the groom and consult among themselves saying: What can we do? Then noticing the presence of Jesus, who is presumably a great prophet, and not daring to ask him directly for help, they go to Mary and ask her: Speak for us, since your Son is coming toward us.

In reality the evangelist's description is much different. In the narrative no one notices the wine running out: neither the servants, nor the head waiter, nor the guests, nor even the groom. And this is a strange thing. Only one person noticed it, Mary; only she.

Why, O Mary, did you notice that there was joy lacking at the banquet? Why did you notice that in us, in the world, there is lacking the joy of the gospel?

Simply *because our Lady has this joy.* And having it in herself, she has a unique sensibility of where it is not present. Full of the Holy Spirit, she instinctively notices when and where the joy of the Spirit is lacking to humankind.

What conclusion can we draw for the Church? That when the Church is full of gospel joy, suddenly it feels drawn toward those that do not have it.

This is the secret of missionary activity. It does not do any good to be concerned above all for others and then perhaps not know what to give them, leading to the question: What ought we do to transmit the gospel?

Essentially, we must become aware of the joy which we are lacking, the joy of faith, and to ask for it from God through the intercession of Mary: Give me, O Lord, some of this wine, give me, O Lord, the fullness of your spirit.

But also we ought to take cognizance of the joy which by the grace of God we do have because when we feel it in ourselves we instinctively notice where it is lacking and our desire to help, to transmit it, is aroused. Each individual has some of the good news, a fact which fills the individual with enthusiasm, which consumes that person with the desire to bring it to others.

Therefore if we do not have this good news, we have nothing to say to our brother and sisters.

The prime source of a missionary Church, of a missionary community, is really to be, as Mary was, full of the Holy Spirit, full of the joy of the gospel.

A Church which prepares the way

The Madonna, when she notices that the wine, the joy, is running out, and that sadness is breaking out, turns to Jesus: "They have no more wine."

She does not put herself at center stage, but instinctively makes Jesus intervene.

Likewise it is not the Church that gives salvation. Likewise also, I do not become missionary by focussing on myself. We must ask for Jesus to intervene, we must put others in contact with him.

Missioning puts people in contact with the source that has first filled me with joy. I want you to participate in that friendship which fills my life, which has changed my sadness into joy, which has revealed LOVE to me.

We notice another curious factor in the incident of Cana. Jesus is already there, invited to the wedding feast, yet up to that moment it's as if he were not there. He is one of so many others, unknown; his divine power has not shown forth, it has not been used and yet it is there.

The Church becomes missionary not by introducing the gospel message forceably into the heart of humankind, because Jesus is already there, he is already invited on his own into the daily routine of each of us, into the festivities of life, into the daily banquet. Jesus is there as one waiting and promising, as seed, as present grace. He waits for each of us to urge him, as Mary did, to make him feel present, to give him space.

The Church is missionary in the measure with which it discovers that Jesus is already waiting in the heart of every man, woman, and child who comes into the world; and he allows each of us to operate and to act by giving him space, by awakening him.

Often the missioning of our communities is boring. It does not move people because we wish to do everything ourselves, we believe that we can do anything at all that is asked of us, whereas it is Jesus who changed water into wine, who gives the joy of the banquet.

The Church, like Mary, is the one who is solicitous, moves forward, speaks to the servants, prepares the way. Jesus, in reality, is already there, and his power is ready to move.

A Church which knows how to be involved

To put in motion the power of Jesus, Mary turns to the servants. In the Greek text, the word is *diaconoi* and it is a very beautiful word: "His mother said to the *diaconoi:* Do whatever he tells you."

These *diaconoi* are given something to do: they fill the jars with water, then they draw water and carry it to the head waiter.

The Madonna could have gone to take the water. However, she incites some of the collaborators, she arouses the activity of the people, she moves them, in such a way that all, as much as possible, get into the activity in which Jesus gives the wine of grace, of joy, of fullness.

The secret of a missionary Church, even a missionary Church in our very midst, among so many who have only a drop of the wine of the gospel and are ready to exhaust the residue of their flasks and then die of thirst or starvation, is to multiply the collaborators, to make it possible for each of us to find others for the task.

How terrible it is when a parish priest says: "How can I be a missionary with all the work I have? It's impossible!"

Sometimes I ask myself: How do you carry the weight of five million people who are in Milan? How do you work with all those who are not coming into the Church?

But it would be absurd and blasphemous to think that the Lord puts all this weight on our shoulders! Not even Mary carried alone the weight of those few invited to Cana, because she looked for collaborators, persons to be involved. And then from one five come along, from five twenty-five come along, and because of these persons of good will, the missionary activity of a Church is multiplied.

Jesus began himself, not by doing everything himself, but by calling the Twelve who, in their time, called others.

The missionary Church is a Church that knows how to involve people; often our communities are not missionaries because they try to leave all the work to some few who arrogate to themselves the prerogative, the importance, the heroism.

"Do whatever he tells you": Mary has the secret of allotting some task to each person. It is a small thing to go to get the water; however, the Lord will do the rest.

The Madonna thus offers us a way for missionary endeavors; she is the evangelizer whom the Pope so frequently recalls to us when he talks about the necessity of a new evangelization in Europe. We will not achieve it by heroic effort on the part of anyone; rather, we must engage ourselves in a gradual, simple, daily movement, each of us in our own way, in the area in which we live, in our own area of expertise, helping each other and performing with simplicity those authentic deeds which allow the joy of the gospel to overflow, collaborating by giving space to Jesus already present.

The good wine needs no recommendation

A final missionary characteristic emerges from that passage of the Gospel where it is stated that the head waiter, after tasting the wine, calls the groom and says: "People usually serve the choice wine first; then when the guests have been drinking awhile, a lesser vintage. What you have done is keep the choice wine until now" (John 2:10).

What does this particular, somewhat humorous, passage in this account suggest to me?

It suggests that the good wine needs no recommendation; it has no dusty labels, no D.O.C.,[1] it does not come from esteemed vineyards. It needs no recommendation because it is good, it is good to the point that all can taste its quality.

We, in our missioning, are not persons who have to, with fear, peddle an inferior product and then timidly resort to prayer that the customers will have the patience to accept it until there is something better.

The good wine needs no recommendation; the joy of the gospel is good for all, it has a distinct taste and whoever tastes it does not ask from what vineyard it came, from which importer, from what area. It is tasty in and of itself, if it is the true joy of the gospel.

Our task—and above all the task of the bishop—is to spread the taste of this joy, which is not the privilege of anyone, not

[1] Controlled Denomination of Origin—authentic trademark for wines.

of this or that particular area, nor of this group; it is the same for all, it is the same evangelical wine and the important thing is that it is authentic, genuine. Then, each of us can be put to work, can start doing our part. Each of us will then spread the joy according to our charism and gifts, not however as our own product or a reserved label, because it is the joy of Jesus, the joy which belongs to the entire Church, to all groups and all areas. The joy of Jesus, by means of which I meet up with a Christian in China, in Korea, in Mexico and I notice by praying together that we both have the same quality, the same taste, the same force, the same capacity to rouse enthusiasm.

Above all, whatever is of consequence to our Lady, to the Church, to the bishop, is really that the authentic joy of the gospel fills our hearts and life with all its truth.

Otherwise, we shall be among those who sell a product without recognizing its worth, without having high esteem for it; we will be among those who attempt to palm off something in bad faith, because they have not tasted and evaluated the product first.

In reality, to pour out on others this joy of the gospel is simply to let overflow the joy within us.

For this reason it is my hope that many will be able to do what you have done in our church, have the experience of that silent, adoring, relationship with the mystery of Jesus, with the mystery of Mary, so as to relish even only a spark of the gospel joy which becomes the motor, the grain, the seed, the germ that cracks the stone, that flourishes everywhere, that does not fear various climates, that is transferred to every area, that knows how to live in every soil, because it vivifies it from within, with the same force that comes from the glory of Christ, from the love of the Father, from the sacrifice of the Son, from the power of the Holy Spirit. A force which above all has filled the heart of Mary with that joy, with that grandeur, with that splendor which we can now prepare ourselves to sing about by honoring in her the first great miracle of the glory of God.

PART II

Quantum Leaps
on the Christian
Educational Journey

School of the Word
on the Gospel according to Mark

ONE

Staying with Jesus

"O Lord, open our hearts to listen to your Word; do not allow us to bring to this listening session our internal troubles, but only the desire to know you as you know us.

"Grant that, through the grace of your Spirit, there may emerge the true questions that you put in our hearts."

The School of the Word is an exercise to teach the method of personal prayer by the use of Sacred Scripture. Consequently it is not just an introduction to the reading or understanding of the Bible, but an introduction to the contemplation of Jesus who speaks to us through the inspired pages of God, the contemplation of the Father in Jesus who is present here and is doing something for the life of each one of us.

In the meetings this year you are following the reading of the Gospel according to Mark by taking some selections which can bring out the definitive moments, quantum leaps on the Christian educational journey. The educational action of God, in fact, goes on even through moments of interruption and the main work of the activity is *Christian conversion.*

Such a conversion is offered again and again in different ages of life and in different situations on our personal human journey.

The texts of the Gospel which have been chosen, clearly show all this in the journey of the apostles as they made their way to follow Jesus.

In the previous meeting you reflected on the desire to change as the fundamental condition for education in the faith beginning with chapter 1 of Mark (vv. 14-20).

This evening we are suggesting a selection from chapter 3 as we ask ourselves: What deeper investigation for conversion does it express for the apostles? What does this difficult and rocky path demand?

I shall try to help you answer by using the exercise of the three steps of *lectio divina:* reading; meditation and reflection; prayer or contemplation.

The reading focuses our attention on the written words by getting a quick look at what was read to us in the passage, what other passages in the Gospel the text reminds us of, what circumstances of place and time emerge, and what the fundamental action of the passage is.

The meditation is the second step and consists in asking ourselves: what has happened among the Twelve who are the central point of the episode? and what does this mean for me, what does it tell me?

The contemplation or prayer we will do in silence with the help of three short questions which I shall suggest. This prayer could then be probed more deeply, for those that might want it, in the sacrament of penance.

The leap which Jesus brings to completion: Mark 3:13-21

Let us re-read the text:

> He then went up the mountain and summoned the men he him-self had decided on, who came and joined him. He named twelve as his companions whom he would send to preach the good news; they were likewise to have authority to expel de-mons. He appointed the Twelve as follows: Simon to whom he gave the name Peter; James, son of Zebedee; and John, the

brother of James (he gave these two the name Boanerges, or "sons of thunder"); Andrew, Philip, Bartholomew, Matthew, Thomas, James son of Alphaeus; Thaddaeus, Simon of the Zealot Party, and Judas Iscariot, who betrayed him. He returned to the house with them and again the crowd assembled, making it impossible for them to get any food whatever. When his family heard of this they came to take charge of him, saying, "He is out of his mind."

In the overall picture, the passage is composed of two scenes, which are contrasted one with the other. The first, from verses 13 to 19, shows an approach to Jesus, a movement toward him: Jesus calls certain persons who go to him and stay with him.

The second, verses 20 and 21, presents a movement of distancing, of estrangement from Jesus, who is thought to be beside himself, detached from reality, out of his mind.

Whereas at the center of the first scene we find the importance of staying with Jesus, at the center of the second scene we find the exclamation, "We can't understand him."

Now what is the Christian conversion, the quantum leap expressed at this point of the journey?

It is the difference between the first and the second way of relating to Jesus.

I want you to note that both of the scenes involve friendly persons, who wish him well: (1) the Twelve, those who will follow him throughout their lives; and (2) his "own," that is, his relatives, his brothers and sisters, those who are not opposed to him.

Whereas the first say, "We are staying with you," the second group conclude, "We do not understand you."

The passage from not understanding the Lord, from not comprehending what he is trying to say, to the expression "We wish to stay with you," designates the specific leap of the Christian conversion which is made obvious here.

In Mark's Gospel there is even a previous scene which it will help to present here. At the beginning of chapter 3, Jesus is so pressed by the people that he needs to get into a boat in order to avoid being crushed.

Now from the scene on the lake there follows the scene on the mountain, which makes up the first part of our excerpt where Jesus calls the Twelve. Finally there is the scene in the house (v. 20), with estrangement from him.

At the center of the three passages (lake, mountain, house) is reported the list of the twelve apostles: from Simon to Judas Iscariot.

It is a sacred list, very ancient, because the Church is founded on the apostles and in fact we repeat their names in the canon of the Mass to affirm our communion with them.

In our meditation last month, you learned about and meditated on the figures of Simon and his brother Andrew—the first two called—and then on the figures of James and John. These are already well known, while the others are mentioned only for the first time in this excerpt.

After having given an overall look, we ask ourselves if this passage recalls others for us.

Certainly chapter 1 comes to mind, which describes the call of Simon and his brother Andrew, of James son of Zebedee and of John his brother. What is the difference between the two calls? What is there "new" in the call of the Twelve? What is this rocky path which Jesus plans to bring to completion for his own who march after him, the quantum leap which he requests?

In chapter 1 there was reference to letting down the nets and following the Lord with confidence, in the somewhat vague hope of becoming fishers of people.

But it is necessary that the first enthusiasm be solidified. The gospel text says that Jesus "appointed the twelve." He gave them a way of being stable, of being participants in what he himself was doing. He appointed them "because they *stayed* with him," in order to send them to preach, in order to give them the power to cast out demons.

This is precisely the fundamental action of the passage. Jesus makes possible the quantum leap in faith by appointing the Twelve because they stood with him and also because they went out to preach and had the power to cast out devils.

The Twelve made up their minds by a choice, a firm commitment to meet others, a new experience of Christian maturity.

If the first departure still had the character of trial, of research, of a bit of curiosity maybe, or an occasion for a little testing (let us see what happens!), this now is a real choice of vocation.

Let us, finally, look at the circumstances of the narrative. I stress three places which I have already mentioned:

The lake where Jesus was preaching, with so many people coming from all parts of Palestine. Jesus is forced to get into the boat.

The mountain, on which—according to the parallel passage from chapter 4 of the Gospel according to Luke—he had retired to pass the night in prayer before calling the Twelve.

The house, to which it is presumed Jesus returned from the lake, the usual center of life for the people. These three places are particularly significant.

In fact, the lake indicates the place of Jesus' preaching and of his charity (he had cured many sick people on the lake); the mountain indicates the place of prayer, of choosing, of great decisions; the house is the place for daily living.

The Lord passes from one to the other, we might say from the pulpit to the altar of everyday life; from the moment of listening to the Word to the moment of profound prayer, to the moment of Eucharist; from prayer to the moment of decision in everyday life.

He passes from one to the other of these realities sanctifying them, meeting people, allowing himself to be provoked by these dramatic human situations that come up to meet him and challenging them in his turn. We can pray to him by saying:

"Lord, also challenge us! Come among us, wherever we may be, see to it that we are found among the crowd, see to it that we are found in the place of prayer, see to it that we are found in the sphere

of daily life! Show us that there is a difference between the one and the other, that we do not have to deny in daily life him whom we desire to recognize on the mountain. Let there be a unity between the different moments of our existence!"

Falling in love with Jesus: points for meditation

We have said that meditation consists really in conjuring up questions about the text. We can ask the Twelve, we can inquire of Peter or John: What did this passage mean for you? What did it mean in your life and what can it imply for mine?

I believe that the apostles would reply to us: for us it would mean putting ourselves definitely on the side of Jesus, challenging the lack of understanding of those who did not understand him even while wishing him well. For you, it could be equivalent to going a bit out of yourselves, to assume a role in the Church, a role of service in the community, a role of duty for life.

If then we wanted to question them a bit more cordially, we might request: Try to describe for us the experience that moved you! I think they would emphasize the experience of "going a bit outside oneself," a bit outside common sense, by explaining it as being enamored with someone, being irresistibly attracted to someone. Before we had a certain esteem for Jesus and we also were somewhat curious; but now we are with him, at his side, we feel that we wish him well, we feel that our heart has been taken up. Falling in love—say the apostles—strictly speaking is not something decided; it just happens. For us it happened just that way because we were chosen; we did not make the decision ourselves. And yet we feel like going after Jesus freely and joyfully, moved by love.

The experience which the apostles live, the new quantum leap comes from the repeated occurrence of falling in love, of dedicating oneself, of allowing oneself to be taken up, of allowing oneself to be seized without conditions.

Questions for our personal prayer

For your silent contemplation I suggest again three questions, following the experience of Peter, John, and the others.

1. Do I agree, do I desire to allow myself to be taken hold of like that? If, before the Lord, he should ask me: do you wish to allow yourself to be grasped by my love, how would I answer him?

Try to see what is stirring within you, in what way you are replying to his question.

2. Am I afraid of the consequences of allowing myself to be taken hold of? It is easy immediately to imagine some of the consequences like this: if I allow myself to be grasped, who knows what choices I would have to carry out. Perhaps to become a priest, a sister. I am a bit frightened. Where might you bring me, Lord? I think the Lord would say: I will bring you to be a Christian, to be with me, to stay with me. To be a Christian, in fact is nothing more than *staying with Christ*. The rest is easy; it will come according to each person's particular calling.

What I want—says the Lord—is that you accept, that you do not fear the consequences of permitting yourself to be seized unconditionally.

3. Have I ever tried anything like it? Have I tried to be with Jesus?

Perhaps we will notice that we have already been seized by him, even if we do not see some of the complete emotional consequences which this implies; sometimes we do notice some of them and these are moments of great joy.

Let us allow this experience to spread within us.

Have I ever tried to be with Jesus? Do I want to try now?

What Jesus asks of you is to stay with him *now*. Jesus wants you to look at him (by rereading the gospel excerpt), to listen to his words which are calling (and if your name were among the Twelve?), to reflect on how you can do this in your life by staying more with him.

"Lord, I thank you because now you are calling me, because the baptismal call means staying with you, because you, with the life of the Church, through the council, through the synod of the laity, are calling me to allow myself to be seized by you!

"Lord, what reason do I have to be afraid? What do I want, what must I overcome, what are the difficulties which cause me to be frightened?

"Lord, give me the taste to stay a little in silence with you!"

TWO

Leaving fear behind
and relying on Jesus

The evangelist Mark this evening gives us the scene concerning the calming of the storm (Mark 4:35-41), which is found immediately after the discussion of the parable about the mustard seed.

We can say that the scene of the storm being calmed by Jesus is a parable "in action," which makes visible the experience described in the parable of the sower (Mark 4:1 ff.). In the parable there is discussion about the seed that falls on rocky ground, that is, about those who accept the Word "with joy but being rootless, they are changeable and thus when some pressure or persecution overtakes them because of the Word, they become disheartened" (v. 17).

Here the apostles, who perhaps held back because they "having roots," experience fear and understand that if they do not cross over this threshold, there is no possibility of entering on the Christian journey.

The central theme of our passage is then the overcoming of fear or timidity. Why do we never make certain decisions, decisions which really are important? Why, even after making them, are we struck with anxiousness and pull back? What is inside of us and what moves Jesus to suggest to us to break away from such fear?

The fear of trusting: Mark 4:35-41

"In rereading an event it is important to know how to divide mentally the stages of the action.

In this passage, there are three periods:

• the preparatory period where there are expressed the conditions of time and place in which the incident occurs;

• the central period, the deed itself: the weather, the reactions of Jesus and the disciples;

• the concluding period, the conclusion of the passage.

Let us consider them separately.

The preparatory period. "That day as evening drew on he said to them, 'let us cross over to the farther shore.' Leaving the crowd, they took him away in the boat in which he was sitting, while the other boats accompanied him" (vv. 35-36).

The time setting is described by the words "That same day." What day? That same day of the parable in which Jesus had spoken of certain realities which he is now using to try his disciples.

"As evening drew on:" the evening is the moment of solitude, of the Word. Remember the two disciples of Emmaus, who say to Jesus: "Stay with us, Lord—the day is practically over" (Luke 24:29).

The evening is also the moment in which people would like to be calm, to be in intimacy and peace.

But Jesus says them: "Let us cross over to the farther shore." Although the disciples might like to rest a bit on their laurels, without having to make involved decisions, the Lord urges them to change venue.

The evangelist adds, "They took him away in the boat in which he was sitting." It is not easy to understand what John wants to say. Perhaps this indicates that Jesus was very tired. According to the description in 4:1, he had boarded a boat already at the beginning of the day, so as to go a distance from the shore, where he had begun to talk to the people. When evening came, then, he was exhausted and wanted to go on his way, just as he was, without going home. They give up a tranquil situation after having won a certain prestige among the people and leave. The disciples have thought about Jesus' strangeness; but in any case, they take him along with them.

O Lord, I also welcome you just as you are, because I too am often tired, exhausted, and so I can understand you.

The central period. ''It happened that a bad squall blew up. The waves were breaking over the boat and it began to sink'' (v. 37).

The main fact is described first of all as a bad squall.

Then the evangelist tells us how Jesus lived through it: ''He was in the stern through it all, sound asleep on a cushion'' (v. 38a).

Finally, he tells us how the apostles behave: ''They finally woke him up and said to him: 'Teacher, does it not matter to you that we are going to drown?' '' (v. 38b).

Let us examine a little bit each of these words: ''A bad squall'' indicates a sudden unexpected disaster, a wind storm, a whirling gale which stirs up the waters. If we have ever had any experience with this, we can imagine what is going on. It is not difficult to imagine the fear which must have grasped the disciples: the little boat is slapped by the waves, the water comes into the boat, they try with their hands to dump the water out so it won't inundate them, their knees shake, their panic increases, disaster is imminent. For this reason they try to awaken Jesus.

But this is a strange thing: why is Jesus sleeping? The boat had to have a kind of poop cover and he must have curled himself up there where he did not feel the waves; he sleeps on a cushion because he is exhausted from his fatigue and he is aware of nothing.

The figure of Jesus asleep recalls the biblical incident of Jonah, sprawled out under the sun, at the time of the storm, in the hold of the vessel. Jonah however was in the hold to hide himself, to flee from God. Jesus, on the other hand, is the very presence of God, he is the absence of fear even in the eye of the cyclone. The disciples however do not understand this and are even irritated, as just we are sometimes irritated when we see someone facing danger joking and laughing.

The disciples waken him with a word of reproof: "Teacher, does it not matter to you that we are going to drown?" The expression is very harsh and it brings to mind that annoyed remark of Martha to Jesus: "Are you not concerned that my sister has left me to do the household tasks all alone?" (Luke 10:40). The apostles seem to be saying: Not only do we not understand you, but we cannot understand how you, in a situation like this, continue to sleep. They are not asking just for moral encouragement, but rather for him to lend them a hand, to help throw out the water from the boat.

We have come to the high point of the passage: "He awoke and rebuked the wind and said to the sea: 'Quiet! Be still!.' The wind fell off and everything grew calm" (v. 39).

"He awoke," in the Greek text, is the verb that brings to mind the resurrection, the rising up, the waking up from sleep of Jesus.

He reproved the wind; he performed, as it were, an exorcism on the evil power which was directly attacking them.

He told the sea, which was turned upside down by the wind, to be quiet, to be calm. "The wind fell off and everything grew calm": this brings to mind some psalms which speak of the power of God: God rebuked the Red Sea, and it was dried up (Ps 106:9); God stilled the roaring of the seas, and the tumult of the peoples (Ps 65:8); God rules over the surging of the sea (Ps 89:10); God hushed the storm to a gentle breeze and the billows of the sea were stilled (Ps 107:29).

At the very instant in which Jesus takes charge of the wind and sea, we must see him, in the light of Scripture, as taking hold of all that is a power against humankind. The sea is an enemy of people because it creates dangers, death, and anxiety when it is agitated by wind. Jesus conquers all the forces of evil and their capacity to put people in desperation. He goes to people who are complaining, "I can do no more!"

It is Christ risen who comes toward us, immersed as we are in the violent storm of history.

Jesus then turned to his disciples: "Why are you so terrified? Why are you lacking in faith?" (v. 40). Literally the Greek text says: "Why are you timid? Don't you have faith any more?"

The question appears strange to us. Really, their fear is of an unexpected disaster! And yet the question is equivalent to a reproof: "Why are you so timid?" Evidently there is something behind this word which signifies fear, timidity, and apprehension, things which appear to us, at most, to be defects, natural reactions. How can Jesus reprove this fear so strongly, connecting it directly with faith?

The words "Why are you timid?" occur only once in the New Testament—besides the parallel texts—namely, in the final passage from the Book of Revelation, where in comparison with the glory of heavenly Jerusalem we find these contrasting words: "But as for the *fearful* [translated as a rule by "cowards," which is really an exact translation] and traitors to the faith, the depraved and murderers, the fornicators and sorcerers, the idol-worshippers and deceivers of every sort—their lot is the fiery pool of burning sulphur, the second death" (Rev 21:8).

The description is dramatic and recalls Dante's hell: in the first circle of the damned there are the cowards, the slothful "despicable to God and enemies to themselves" (*Divina Commedia: Inferno* 3. 60 ff.). Among them the poet sees the shadow of "the one who through his cowardice made the great refusal," one who had fear of speaking his mind—perhaps Celestine V or perhaps Pilate. A seemingly marginal fear forced the decision, even though it was a decision not to decide.

This is why the passage from Revelation places the timid among the unbelievers, the traitors to the faith, the depraved, the murderers, the fornicators and sorcerers, the idol-worshippers, the deceivers. Notice that the same relationship in Revelation between the timid and the traitors is found in Jesus' statement: "Do you still not have faith?"

What we must understand this evening is that the fear of the disciples is not only a physical fear, timidity, but it is the fear of trusting in Jesus.

The disciples fear placing their trust completely and they go back to calculating their own resources; but they realize that they can't manage and fear breaks in.

Before that they had not tested him: they said yes to the Lord when they were among his listeners with John the Baptist; then a second yes when Jesus had suggested to them, "Come after me."

However, it is at this point in their lives that they are put to the test, a very serious test. Their yes was not deeply rooted and it was necessary that they be shaken and sifted by trials. For every yes in life, every yes which is meant to be serious (yes to Jesus, yes to a friend, yes to a lady, yes to a man, yes to a daunting task) one must know how to survive the test, whatever might be one's fatigue or the criticism, the scorn, the aloneness, the nonapproval of others.

We must know how to enter into the turbulence of fear; we must learn to know the moment in which I look at my own power and understand that I cannot cope. Saying "I am not doing any of this through my own resources," is an attitude much more serious than it seems, especially since it seems correct. If I stop and go home, I have already fallen. If I forget my confidence in Jesus, if I forget the mysterious attraction which brought me to choose a task, a person, a friendship which motivated me to make a promise, if I forget that life is deceived by trusting myself, I am finished.

This situation of fear, when cultivated and accepted, is connected with disbelief—when it concerns existential decisions about Jesus and the serious realities of life—because faith, by its nature, dissipates fear.

Faith and confidence are not the same thing.

Timidity is a sign of little faith; it comes from giving in to our calculating and diffident nature, from being wrapped up in ourselves and then tearing from its roots the confidence with which the yes was spoken.

There is a dangerous, even if necessary, moment of transition in which it is necessary to explain to ourselves that, if we do not free ourselves from the fear caused by confiding in ourselves, we go backwards and we will not make this decision or any other great decisions of life.

Wishing to deepen ultimately the significance of the words of Jesus—"Why are you fearful? Do you still not have faith?"— we can say that incredulity is inadequate understanding of the hidden story of the kingdom of God, described in the parables. The kingdom of God is there but it is not seen; Jesus sleeps but he is present and there is no fear if we have entrusted ourselves to him. Anyone who does not understand this hidden story of the kingdom of God will also not understand the journey of Jesus to the cross, as happened in the case of Peter. He or she will not understand that God is present with us in all the hidden and difficult moments of our existence.

The question here then is of understanding or not understanding the manner of the presence of Jesus in our life.

The concluding period. "A great awe overcame them at this. They kept saying to one another, 'Who can this be that the wind and the sea obey him?' " (v. 41).

We have just now been discussing worry (*timore*), not fear (*paura*); the Greek word is totally different. At first they were "timid," then they had "great fear," that is reverential, religious fear, fear which brings them to realize they are standing in the presence of a mystery. On the one hand there is reverence and on the other the fullness of confidence in the affection of God.

The opposite of timidity—the gospel words inform us—is neither presumption, nor impudence, nor recklessness, but rather reverential fear for the great tenderness with which God is close to us and that, once it is experienced, puts to flight timidity and fear while producing peace, calm, serenity, and joy. There is a feeling that someone is present and is much bigger than we are; that the little things which we are living through bring us to a reality greater than our experience, to the taste of a presence that is holy, tender, affectionate, capable of never leaving us.

Apropos of meditation and contemplation

I would like, at this point, to suggest to you a question which can serve as your meditation, as a more specific reflection on your life.

How and when is this fear expressed in me? Do I sometimes notice it on my journey of faith? How and when is it expressed in my actions, so that others have seen and judged it and, then, held me back from doing things which I thought right? How and when has fear been expressed in my heart, when I alone have found it and felt badly because I allowed myself to be overcome by it?

This fundamental question must then become *contemplation*, must be transformed into a simple conversation with Jesus. Look at Jesus from the point of view of the disciples, from one's own personal point of view, from the point of view of Jesus himself, and say:

"Lord, through my contemplation of you who by awakening yourself again from sleep and having risen from the dead, have given me confidence, free me, I beg you, from my worries (timori), *my fears* (paure), *my indecisions, the obstacles to my important choices, to my friendships, to my forgiveness, to my relationships with others, to my acts of courage in manifesting my faith. Take away my obstacles, O Lord!"*

I invite you to continue for the entire month with these reflections by dedicating some moments either among yourselves, in parishes, or personally. Continue and exert yourselves in the contemplation which we have introduced, by stopping to look at Jesus, by standing in silence before him or by exchanging with one another the reflections which he himself might suggest to you.

You could also think of an act of courage to undertake as you are prompted by faith. This should not be an act of effrontery, of bragging, but a gesture, personal or of the group, which comes from the certainty that Jesus frees the heart and makes spontaneous and joyful the act of courage done through faith.

Virgin Mary—who had no fear, and entrusted herself to him by saying, "Lord, I do not fear, but may your word be fulfilled in me!"—give us the ability to participate in every moment of life with the joy of your unconditional faith.

THREE

Facing opposition

Jesus departed from there and returned to his own part of the
country followed by his disciples. When the sabbath came he
began to teach in the synagogue in a way that kept his large
audience amazed. They said: "Where did he get all this? What
kind of wisdom is he endowed with? How is it that such miraculous deeds are accomplished by his hands? Is this not the
carpenter, the son of Mary, a brother of James and Joses and
Judas and Simon? Are not his sisters our neighbors here?" They
found him too much for them. Jesus' response to all this was:
"No prophet is without honor except in his native place, among
his own kindred, and in his own house." He could work no
miracle there, apart from curing a few who were sick by laying
hands on them, so much did their lack of faith distress him.

He made the rounds of the neighboring villages instead, and
spent his time teaching. He summoned the twelve and began
to send them out two by two, giving them authority over unclean spirits. He instructed them to take nothing on their journey but a walking stick—no food, no traveling bag, not a coin
in the purses in their belts. They were, however, to wear san-
dals. "Do not bring a second tunic," he said, and added:
"Whatever house you find yourself in, stay there until you leave
the locality. If any place will not receive you or hear you, shake
its dust from your feet in testimony against them as you leave"
(Mark 6:1-11).

Preliminary remarks

The passage of the Gospel of Mark, proposed for our meditation, has need of some preliminary remarks.

All of us are conditioned by the judgments made on us by other people and at times this conditioning is so strong that it prevents us from doing what we ought.

This attitude is serious because it causes a crisis in one's sincerity on the way to conversion. That is why the courage to confront opposition through faith is essential for the Christian pilgrimage.

How many times I have listened to the difficulties that young people have in their lives, whether in school or at work, or the difficulty they face in persevering in the life of prayer because of the opinions of some of their companions on matters of faith or Christian practice!

From this observation there comes the question which becomes our prayer for this meeting: How, O Lord, do you confront this conditioning that comes from the negative judgments of others? How are you teaching us to confront it? How did you educate the apostles and us also to overcome such obstacles? How do you educate us to bring about a new conversion in courage and freedom in faith?

I would like to observe that even Jesus is sensitive to what is being said about him. At Caesarea Philippi, for example, he will ask his disciples, "Who do people say that I am?" and then he will ask again, "And you, who do you say that I am?" (Mark 8:27-30 and parallel passages).

On the other hand it is not socially possible to ignore entirely things that others say about us. To do so, we would have to close ourselves up in a monastery and yet, even then we would be pursued by the judgments of people about our conduct.

The problem, therefore, is not how to escape conditioning from judgments, but how not to be slaves to it.

Jesus appears in our passage profoundly and negatively influenced by the reactions of the crowd: his words and actions are not understood, he is rejected, and therefore he experiences amazement, suffers, is astonished. It is plainly said that Jesus "could work no miracle there" (v. 5), leaving the impression thereby that even his ability to work miracles was hamstrung because of the poor reception of the people.

Something like that happens also to us. For example, if we speak in public and we notice hostility or indifference the words become difficult to speak, the trend of our discourse is lost, it loses its zip. Jesus, whose overwhelming power of curing comes to a halt at that moment as if blocked, understands us and we can address ourselves to him saying: Jesus, you who understand us in our conditioning by the judgments of others about us, help us to read the passage presented this evening, so that we can be illuminated by the way you conducted yourself.

The reaction of Jesus when challenged: Mark 6:1-11

I distinguish in the text from Mark four successive components:

- Jesus teaches;
- the people are surprised;
- Jesus reacts;
- the consequences for the disciples at the action of Jesus.

Let us reread each of those components, which we will then take back for the silence of the meditation and the Eucharistic adoration.

1. *Jesus teaches.* The evangelist writes: "He departed from there, and returned to his own part of the country" (v. 1).

This note is important because often it is more difficult to have the courage of faith when we are surrounded by acquaintances and people have put us in a cage with preconceived ideas; we feel less free. I am thinking of youth groups who are not able to grow because of a closing off of feelings on the part of those who condition them. In a strange environment we are more free, less ill at ease.

Jesus gives a perfect example of a problem which happened to him in his country, in the midst of his own people, in his own town. The text adds that "the disciples followed him." Even they are watchful and disturbed by what is happening. "When the sabbath came, he began to teach in the synagogue" (v. 2a).

Jesus keeps to the program of sticking with the traditions of the people, according to which on the day of the Sabbath all had to assemble in the synagogue. Without any disruption or noisy gesture, he goes, sits on the ground with the people, and listens in silence to the reading of the scroll, which is done with great solemnity (Luke 4:16ff.). Then when the scroll is rolled up, the head of the synagogue, noticing the presence of Jesus who had been in the school of John the Baptist, asks him for a word of exhortation. He gets up and begins the sermon which we know from the Gospel of Luke: "Today this Scripture passage is fulfilled in your hearing" (Luke 4:21).

2. *The people are surprised.* We are now at the second component of the passage.

"Many, upon hearing him, were *amazed*" (v. 2b). The Greek word means to be struck by something great, something unexpected. It is used, for example, to describe the amazement of Mary and Joseph when they found Jesus in the Temple: "Why have you done this to us? We have been looking for you!" (cf. Luke 2:41ff.).

The people finally are amazed and express their surprise with exclamations, even though customarily there is silence in the synagogue. "Where did he get all this? Where did he get such wisdom and miraculous powers?" (Matt 13:54ff.). Let us try to examine the words which are whispered as the feelings, at first attentive, begin to get nervous, as Jesus notes.

Evidently he spoke in a simple manner, because all understood, and at the same time what he said was so original, so fresh, so spontaneous, so new, so little repetitious of old ideas that the crowd is asking where he learned what he was teaching, from whom he heard it.

Now we can make a reflection. It is very proper to inquire of Jesus, "Where did he get all this?" In fact, the first characteristic of Christian courage, the characteristic of expressing freely in public one's faith, comes from having something inside one; the words which are spoken are not the fruit of reading, of listening to a sermon, but are rather words lived by, words heard before, words which have become one's own through faith.

This first characteristic of Christian courage makes our testimony really be *ours*, it jumps up from our heart like a mountain spring, it springs up like water. That is why the quantum leap previously asked for is that of *being with Jesus*, of meditating on his word, of listening to it, of contemplating him so that he is rooted deeply inside us like seed in the ground. Then the courage of faith automatically springs up because the seed, when it is well rooted in the ground, irresistibly gives birth to the sprout.

It is *staying with Jesus*, contemplating in silence his gospel, the entrusting oneself to him by overcoming one's fears, performing little acts of confidence in him, that is fundamental. Of me too it could be said: Where did he get all this? How is it, from inside you, there is this force, this simplicity, this wisdom?

In the passage from Mark, therefore, the people suddenly go from admiration to criticism to distrust. "Is this not the carpenter, the son of Mary, a brother of James and Joses and Judas and Simon? Are not his sisters our neighbors here?" (v. 3).

The people at this point make a judgment about Jesus: he is poor like all the others, he has lived a life like all the others, from him there has been nothing new. If he had been a great prophet who came from Jerusalem, who had studied in the schools of the capital, it would be different, but since he is just one of the country people, it is useless to listen to him.

Jesus is already studied and enclosed in an obtuse, wretched, judgment which offends him, which does not understand him, which disregards him, which closes its eyes to truth.

Here one sees the stupidity of judgments which are made in the presumption of criticizing our faith or our Christian commitment, by attacking our sincerity and preventing us from growing.

Finally the gospel account says, "And they found him too much for them." These are very strong words; from that moment disparagement blocks the moral road and the road of faith. Jesus becomes right away an obstacle because the people are unable to believe that God, great and immense as he is, acts with weak and poor instruments. And this is the great scandal which is opposed to the gospel: God cannot act through the poor, the humble, the simple, those without standing. God's way of acting must of necessity be different. In the judgments of the people there is indeed revealed ignorance about God, in effect atheism, the lack of understanding of who God is and the desire then to reduce him to one's own standards.

The judgments which tend to terrify, to alarm, to trap, are a corollary of lies and deceptions, of wrong interpretations, which, if taken seriously, tend to confuse us, to hem us in, preventing the truth about ourselves from emerging.

3. *Jesus reacts.* We have already indicated how Jesus faced the dispute. We return to this point by commenting on the verse, "So much did their lack of faith distress him" (v. 6a).

Jesus first of all reacts with sorrowful amazement, with painful surprise: in fact, he is found here confronted with the very terrible attitude which is the inability to put one's trust in God, to believe that God can do something really big in our little areas of life, that God is manifested even in the humble circumstances of daily life.

Jesus comes up against this tremendous existential frustration, which is the source of the negative judgments upon those who, on the other hand, believe in and place their trust in him.

After the surprise, he experiences a kind of blockade; his love, his desire to heal is impeded. This must have been a terrible suffering for him.

This is really why he looks for a reason: "Jesus' response to all this was: 'No prophet is without honor except in his native place, among his own kindred, and in his own house' " (v. 4). The reason given by Jesus is the same one that we tried to pick out when listening to the people: the meanness of their hearts and their backgrounds. Hearts and backgrounds closed to the true action of God, not the shallowness of some sixteen-year-old religious young man who sees this action only in great deeds, great undertakings, in amazing and flamboyant things. The real activity of God is manifested also in simplicity, in poverty, in humility, in the simple and lovable appearance of Jesus of Nazareth.

By giving a reason, Jesus refocuses the negative judgments, he shakes them up and down, he liberates them.

Finally, he continues as before and even before that: "He made the rounds of the neighboring villages instead, and spent his time teaching" (v. 6b). The conflict, far from causing him to change his program, far from having suggested to him that it should be presented differently and that he should find more ostentatious forms, or solemn ones, to make the people understand that he came from on high, simply leads him to continue as before. He moves ahead therefore in the evangelical, apostolic, simple, profoundly sure manner of his mission.

Jesus reacts by passing through these four stages: astonishment, suffering of feeling blocked in his love for humankind, search for a reason which redirects the judgments, certainty of having to continue to teach as he had always done.

4. *The consequences for the disciples at the action of Jesus.* The confrontation not only results in their following Jesus in his teaching, but also in moving him to send the Twelve, because he has fortified their courage.

He begins by sending the disciples two by two, giving them power over unclean spirits (v. 7). He sends them to do good and he desires that they be, like himself, without show, without pomp. "He instructed them to take nothing on their journey but a walking stick—no food, no traveling bag, not a coin in the purses in their belts" (v. 8).

In poverty and with great freedom of heart: ''If any place will not receive you or hear you, shake its dust from your feet in testimony against them as you leave'' (v. 11).

Jesus, when confronted, did not retreat into himself, but multiplied his activity.

It would be well, for our purpose here, to recall the examples of the suffering and persecuted Church, which were heard in the last synod of bishops! We were able to gain some insight into how much strength rises in the Church and in the faithful from confrontation and martyrdom.

The joy of the testimonies coming from the bishops of Churches where Christians are in difficulty electrified all the other bishops and afforded one of the most beautiful moments of Catholic communion at the synodal gathering.

Questions for meditation and contemplation

Now that the rereading of the passage is completed, the time for meditation and contemplation of Jesus in the Eucharist begins, the moment for asking him, on the basis of the gospel passage, to allow his message to surface for each of us.

To help you, I suggest four simple and useful questions for an examination of conscience and for prayer:

Where and when do I feel conditioned by the things people say about me because of my faith? Let us try to recall the places and situations in which we felt most conditioned by the judgments or the criticisms of others about our activity.

How do I usually react in these cases? Do I tighten up, do I get irritable, do I get angry, do I take the criticism and keep silent? Or do I get frightened, do I not do as much as I wanted to do, do I change my program? Do I act as Jesus did?

How do I evaluate my reactions now, as I pray before the Eucharist, in the light of those of Jesus in the gospel message?

O Lord, what should I do on the next occasion? What do you suggest to me so that on that next occasion I can conduct myself as I desire?

FOUR

Facing and welcoming
the discourse about the Cross

Tonight we will reflect on the main passage of Mark's Gospel which we can express with the words: facing and welcoming the discourse about the cross.

After having said yes to following Jesus, after having passed some tests with him and having overcome fear, now comes the clarification of the way, which is not necessarily identified with a vocation in the strict sense of the word, but concerns all those who are pledged, through the grace of baptism, to the life of faith.

Facing and welcoming the discourse about the cross means facing up to the discourse of Jesus about the kingdom of God and accepting it as divine logic, not simply as bare fact.

This is why the passage Mark 8:27-33 is important. And I would like to recall also what St. Paul says to the Corinthians: "The message of the cross is complete absurdity to those who are headed for ruin, but to us who are experiencing salvation it is the power of God" (1 Cor 1:18). Here is a discourse which is capable of dividing people, of causing certain people to shrug their shoulders and to deny it, as others come to affirm it saying, "Here is God at work."

In our text, Peter is the one who in the beginning shrugged his shoulders, did not accept the discourse of Jesus, but did somewhat later accompany him and become an apostle, a holy man, the rock of the Church. The difficulty experienced by Peter is a symbol of all of our difficulties as we face the discourse about the cross. A similar difficulty was seen in the case of St. Paul himself: when he began to preach, he limited himself to speaking about Jesus as an extraordinary individual who did good, and he neglected to talk about the crucifixion. In fact, at Athens, a place of refined culture, he preached in a wise, philosophical manner without ever mentioning the cross. But his discourse was a failure and the Apostle left Athens and went to Corinth with a grieving and frustrated heart saying: What happened? How did it ever happen?

Then he realized that he made a mistake in hedging on the discourse about the cross and wrote about this in the First Letter to the Corinthians, which is a splendid hymn on the wisdom of the cross.

The Quantum leap: the way of the Cross (Mark 8:27-33)

Then Jesus and his disciples set out for the villages around Caesarea Philippi. On the way he asked his disciples this question: "Who do people say that I am?" They replied, "Some, John the Baptizer, others, Elijah, still others, one of the prophets." "And you," he went on to ask, "who do you say that I am?" Peter answered him, "You are the Messiah!" Then he gave them strict orders not to tell anyone about him. He began to teach them that the son of Man had to suffer much, be rejected by the elders, the chief priests, and the scribes, be put to death, and rise three days later.

He said these things quite openly. Peter then took him aside and began to remonstrate with him. At this he turned around and, eyeing the disciples, reprimanded Peter: "Get out of my sight, you satan! You are not judging by God's standards but by man's."

This narrative is clearly divided into two parts: the first comprises the questions of Jesus to the disciples; the second, the discourse on the cross given by Jesus and the negative reaction of Peter.

We wish, first of all, to analyze the different parts of the event, by rereading the text.

Then I will suggest some points for meditation, by trying to understand what the discourse about the cross means for us.

Finally I will offer some questions which may help you during the silence.

The purpose of the School of the Word—I want to stress again—is to have each of us come in living contact with the person of Jesus who throughout the pages of the gospel speaks to us even today and is present in our midst as long as we listen to his word.

The geographical context of the passage from Mark is quickly given to us: Jesus leaves with his disciples for the villages around Caesarea Philippi. This is an area which is not named anywhere in the Gospels, and was inhabited, at least so it seems, by pagans. Jesus is not known in those places and no one takes any notice of him. That is why he can calmly busy himself with his disciples by dedicating himself to their formation.

The interrogation. Jesus molds them not only with regard to his teachings but with practical exercises by bringing out something important in each of his apostles. At this point, he asks a very decisive question: "Who do people say that I am?" (v. 27).

The reply is given by recalling some people of God, persons who speak in the name of the Lord, like John the Baptist, Elijah, and other prophets. The people interpret Jesus correctly, putting him in the category of religious and prophetic people: he is a man who is among us in the name of God.

The repetition. He still insists, "But *you,* who do you say that I am?" (v. 29). How far precisely does your recognition of me go? We can imagine that with the new question there followed a silence which was a bit embarrassing or fearful on the part of the apostles. At a certain point, then, comes Peter's sudden inspiration: "You are the Christ." The others are partial prophets, mediators for particular times in history; but you are the absolute mediator, you are the key in history, you are the one who will later take it upon himself to recapitulate the preceding history and explain what will come.

The reply of Peter is super, it is a great act of faith. Yet Jesus is not satisfied. He does not reject the affirmation, but he prefers that there be no talk about him before he had clearly clarified what must be understood by saying "the Christ." The Sermon on the Mount comes to mind: "None of those who cry out, 'Lord, Lord,' will enter the kingdom of God, but only the one who does the will of my Father in heaven" (Matt 7:21). The one who calls me Christ cannot think that he is saved if he does not understand the meaning of those words.

He began to teach. Let us go to the second part of the passage, on which we want to meditate very attentively. Jesus began a new teaching, never given before, a teaching now which he will continue in the future. He pronounces this discourse in chapter 8 of Mark, will repeat it in chapter 9, and will repeat it in chapter 10 in almost identical words. In other ways, he will return to the theme when he goes to Jerusalem as the time of the passion draws near.

"He began to teach them that the Son of Man had to suffer much" (v. 31).

In the hearts of the apostles there is created a perplexity, because "the Son of Man" is a title drawn from a famous passage of the prophet Daniel, in which the Son of Man appeared in a cloud in the heaven, like the glorious end of the journey of the people of God, like the resolution of the historical tragedies in a glorification of divine work (Dan 7:13-14).

According to Jesus, however, this Son of Man "must suffer much." The words are tough, even if they remain somewhat vague, and they invoke sorrow; above all Christ does not have the destiny of success, of being able to turn all in his favor.

And the suffering becomes specific: he will suffer in the sense that he will be *rejected*. It is cruel for a person to be despised; we can have some painful illness and yet others stay close to us, they accept us. The suffering of Jesus is more sorrowful because here he is separated, ostracized, refused by the people.

It is not a refusal by sinners, by thoughtless people who do not know God, but by three categories of people: the elders, the chief priests, and the scribes. In terms understandable to us today, the rejection was by the political, religious, intellectual, and cultural powers. He was banished by all those who represent the influential, the public and civil agents of responsibility.

These are really words which profoundly disturb the apostles.

"Then put to death." This is not just a contrast similar to that of the prophet Jeremiah who was then rehabilitated and given honor. No, Jesus is absolutely eliminated, and his mission is forthwith shut off.

"And rise three days later." Here the discourse is most difficult and goes beyond all possible experiences. Why suffer so much for us only to rise afterward? What is the meaning of "rise"?

Jesus "said these things openly" (v. 32). These words, poured into the bewildered hearts of the disciples, make them think that perhaps the Master was really hinting in a veiled way at the theme. They begin to understand, for example, the previous parables: the kingdom of God is like a seed which is trampled on, suffocated by thorns, pecked at by birds. Jesus spoke of the Word, but he was speaking also of himself, of his way of the cross. The kingdom of heaven is like a mustard seed, which no one bothers about, which is thrown on the ground, and some grew unexpectedly. Jesus was speaking of himself (Mark 4:1-7, 30-32).

The discourse about the kingdom of God can be made clear: it is the discourse of Christ, the Messiah, the Lord, the Savior, who suffers from the poverty and the irrelevance already associated with the kingdom.

Jesus will continually refer back, during the rest of his life, to this theme and he will recall it after his death, in particular in the Gospel of Luke when speaking to his disciples at Emmaus: " 'What little sense you have! How slow you are to believe all that the prophets have announced! Did not the Messiah have to undergo all this so as to enter into his glory?' Beginning with Moses and all the prophets, he interpreted for them every passage of Scripture which referred to him" (Luke 24:25-27).

This is indeed a discourse of few words: suffer, be despised, be killed, rise. It is a synopsis and can be expanded by recalling the teaching of Moses and some of the prophets. It is the Christian discourse *par excellence:* it reads the entire Bible as summed up in Jesus crucified and risen. " 'Recall those words I spoke to you when I was still with you; everything written about me in the law of Moses and the prophets and Psalms had to be fulfilled.' Then he opened their minds to the understanding of the Scriptures. He said to them: 'Thus it is written that the Messiah must suffer and rise from the dead on the third day' " (Luke 24:44-46). This is the way in which the Scriptures present Jesus. This is the meaning of the words, "He said these things quite openly" (Mark 8:32).

The early Church will take it up, Paul will repeat it, and it forms the central affirmation of the Creed: "For our sake he was crucified under Pontius Pilate; he suffered, died, and was buried. On the third day he rose again in fulfillment of the Scriptures."

When we say that Jesus is the solution for all human problems, perhaps we really do not understand it. Jesus resolves human problems by means of his suffering, his death, his resurrection, and only if we follow him on the road with confident dedication can we truthfully make that statement.

"Peter took him aside and began to remonstrate with him." This is the only instance in the Gospels where Jesus is rebuked by an apostle. A similar event occurred in the house at Bethany, when Martha reproached the Master because her sister was not helping her; but Martha in that instance is nervous, irritated, and spits out the first thing that comes to her mind.

Peter, on the other hand, has made a very clear profession of faith. However I am not finished on that point.

What does Peter say in remonstrating with Christ? I think of the argument that we find in the Book of Job: "Why did you bring me forth from the womb? I should have died and no eye have seen me!" (Job 10:18). Or perhaps in the words of the disciples from Emmaus: "We were hoping that he was the one who would set Israel free, that he would have given us victory, triumph, and not indeed anything like all this" (cf. Luke 24:21).

Peter would have noticed that Jesus was losing his friends, that, since he was speaking in this way, he would not be known, that he was presenting an image of himself and of God that the apostles would not have accepted. God, Peter was saying, is the God of glory, a God who has the ability to overcome his enemies, while you are speaking of being despised, of losing.

We are at the dramatic moment of the discourse on the cross, because everyone, even an ecclesiastical person like Peter, wants a God who is only successful, triumphant; they do not accept the seed which falls to the ground and dies, the leaven in the bread, the mustard seed.

"At this Jesus turned around and, eyeing the disciples, reprimanded Peter: Get out of my sight, you satan!" (v. 33).

It is unheard of in the Gospels that the Lord called anyone "satan." He had never done that, not even with the worst sinners, not even with the scribes and Pharisees. This one word of his is incredible, cutting.

What did he intend to say? He intended to say that Peter, by rejecting the discourse on the cross, refuses to open for humanity the ways of life. He is just like Satan who does not want the good of humankind, because he is in principle a murderer, a monster, he is the one who opens to humankind the ways of death.

And there's more: You, Peter—continues Jesus—you believe you are interpreting God, but my God, my Father loves humanity to the point of giving his Son even to death. God the Father loves humanity so much that he gives his Son even if humanity rejects him; he even offers pardon to humanity at the same time.

Here there is at stake the very image of God; Peter's image is still to some extent distorted, caricaturized, confused, and even in us, it is a bit distorted by often bringing us to false conclusions about life.

We who profess in the Creed "God the Father Almighty, creator of heaven and earth," do not have the true image of God until we take the Christian gospel step of welcoming the way of the cross.

"You are not judging by God's standards but by man's." Here one recalls the great words of Isaiah: "For my thoughts are not your thoughts, nor are your ways my ways" (55:8).

Peter wants to twist the ways of God; he says it like it ought to be, like God is expected to be. But it is God who reveals himself to humanity: I am for you, I am with you, I am Jesus crucified and risen.

God is identified with the figure of the Crucified One risen, not with some victorious idol, some symbol of comfort, some sort of pseudo-messianic promise. God is identified only with Jesus, and him crucified, dead, and risen.

The Risen One is the victor, it is he who has overcome all the tests, who has therefore conquered the battle of life by his passion and death.

Points for meditation:
the fundamental Christian discourse

After having reread the selection from Mark, I suggest some thoughts for your personal meditation.

What is this discourse about the cross, to which Jesus gives such importance and on which he does not yield even an inch, not even to please Peter who loves him so much?

It is the discourse through which our happiness, our joy, passes.

Jesus wants our happiness and God does everything that we might be happy. The discourse on the cross is therefore not to be identified with a reality which simply exalts mortification, renunciation, unsuccessfulness as such, failure, and defeat as a kind of a losing mysticism.

It starts with the love of God for us, with the fact that God wants for us the way of life and wishes to fill us with his goods. Yet, the way of life is threatened by the way of death, the way of sin, of Cain killing Abel, of the tower of Babel, all of which separates humans from God and neighbor; the way of death destroys society, threatens deterioration and the general decay of humankind, as described in the first chapters of the Book of Genesis.

The way of life is that of Jesus wiping out the ways of sin, hunger, injustice, and social and political corruption, and becomes the life of faith, of conversion, of the cross: it is to entrust oneself to Jesus with eyes closed, to entrust oneself to his salvation plan, to believe that he died because he loves human beings to the end, to render irrefutable the salvific love of God for us. To entrust oneself to Jesus who, because he wants us close to himself, makes us capable of walking with him, is to participate a little in his cross which is, in reality, the way of life.

The way of the cross does not repudiate reason by uttering sentimentalities and absurdities; it is the way of the life of God, which Jesus causes to travel through the paths of an unjust, fragmented, and divided humanity, in the meanderings of a decadent culture, of a corrupt society.

The way of the cross is the way of salvation in the midst of this society; it is the way of departure from the slavery of Egypt, it is the way of Abraham, it is the way of the people who were returning from Exile.

It is the way of happiness, following Christ to the utmost in the often dramatic circumstances of daily living; it is the way which does not fear failure, difficulties, margination, solitude, because it fills our hearts with the fullness of Jesus.

It is the way of peace, of joy, of serenity, of dominion over oneself. It alone brings humanity back to justice.

When we conscientiously undertake this way, it permits us to become real Christians, to accept all those messages of life which, although they are obscure to the world, resonate in history and fuse into one, creating a huge river of peace and justice which bring joy to the city of God.

Finally this is the fundamental discourse of the Christian life, which reconstructs the outline of existence by making us go unharmed through the fire and flames of corruption and persecution. It is the only and essential Christian discourse, and the Church repeats it continually in the Eucharist which constitutes the center of the liturgical year with Easter.

Start of the contemplative silence

We will conclude with three useful questions for reflection in our silence before the Lord.

Are there any signs in me of limited understanding of the discourse on the cross? That is, do I feel a bit like Peter who does not accept, who cannot understand?

What are these signs? Obviously the question here is not of limited intellectual understanding since what is important is to understand with the heart, and to entrust oneself to God. Rather, I think there are some characteristic states of soul that we can find in our lives: for example, a discontent spread over me and others, a general pessimism about existence, an easy irritability. These are signs of persons who have not accepted the discourse of the cross.

Do I see in myself the signs of understanding the discourse on the cross? They are: peace especially in difficulties, joy in solitude, readiness for mortification, happiness in making some renunciation without fear of losing something. The capacity, briefly, to enter upon the way of the cross as the way of life, of happiness.

Are these signs predominant in me?

What sign, what denial, do we wish to propose to ourselves to show that we welcome the way of the cross of Jesus?

Your gathering here to pray and to reflect in silence indicates already that you are following the way of the cross, that you want to live Lent well.

"Grant us, O Lord, to understand what other signs you ask of our lives so that we do not reject your Word, as Peter did, but that we, like John, might become listeners and followers of the way of the cross which leads to the way of Easter."

FIVE

"And he confirmed the message"

I am happy that for this last meeting of the School of the Word for this pastoral year we have assembled here all the young people who on the first Thursdays of the past months have been meditating on the educational way which Jesus, in Mark's Gospel, brings to completion for his disciples.

Now, together we want to contemplate the finale of Mark. Properly speaking that finale is not attributed to that evangelist but was drawn up by the early Christian community, because of a desire to offer a catechetical compendium on Easter and also on the Church of that time and all times.

The excerpt concerns us in a particular way. In fact, whereas the other passages of the gospel refer to events of the past, this one describes the history of the Church for all times starting with the resurrection of Jesus.

A reading from Mark 16:9-20

First of all let us reread the text, dividing it into its fundamental parts.

> Jesus rose from the dead early on the first day of the week. He first appeared to Mary Magdalene, out of whom he had cast seven demons. She went to announce the good news to his followers, who were now grieving and weeping. But when they

heard that he was alive and had been seen by her, they refused to believe it. Later on, as two of them were walking along on their way to the country, he was revealed to them completely changed in appearance. These men retraced their steps and announced the good news to the others; but the others put no more faith in them than in Mary Magdalene. Finally, as they were at table, Jesus was revealed to the Eleven. He took them to task for their disbelief and their stubbornness, since they had put no faith in those who had seen him after he had been raised.

Then he told them: ''Go into the whole world and proclaim the good news to all creation. The man who believes in it and accepts baptism will be saved; the man who refuses to believe in it will be condemned. Signs like these will accompany those who have professed their faith: they will use my name to expel demons, they will speak entirely new languages, they will be able to handle serpents, they will be able to drink deadly poison without harm, and the sick upon whom they lay their hands will recover.'' Then, after speaking to them, the Lord Jesus was taken up into heaven and took his seat at God's right hand. The Eleven went forth and preached everywhere. The Lord continued to work with them throughout and confirm the message through the signs which accompanied them.

It is not difficult to discern that this long narrative consists of three parts:

• *the first part* gives a summary of the appearances of Jesus after his death and resurrection: to Mary Magdalene, to the two disciples, to the other eleven;

• *the second part* reports the words of the Lord's mandate, the mission and the signs of that mission. This part is the main point of this entire passage, especially the command, ''proclaim the good news'';

• *the third part* describes the concluding events.

As I said, we have here a little catechism on the resurrection which refers to the more detailed accounts in, for example, the final passages of Luke and John. Think of the appearance of Jesus to Mary Magdalene (John 20:11-18); the selection about the two disciples from Emmaus (Luke 24:13-35); the appearance of the Lord to the apostles (Luke 24:36 ff.).

The words of Jesus also have a parallel in the Gospel of Matthew: "Go, therefore, and make disciples of all the nations. Baptize them in the name of the Father, and of the Son, and of the Holy Spirit. Teach them to carry out everything I have commanded you" (Matt 28:19-20).

The passage which we have selected recalls in it many other things for us and is a synthesis of those words of Jesus which still today constitute the Church in the state of mission. He, here, as the definitive Lord of history, indicates the way and the direction for the Church.

The three appearances

We can now ponder more specifically each of the parts of this excerpt trying to understand them better, then asking certain questions.

The three appearances are placed right in the center of the activities: the Risen One appears to Mary Magdalene, but when she tells this to the disciples they do not want to believe; he appears to two of them, and not even they wanted to believe; he appears to the Eleven and he reproves them for their disbelief.

Their apathy in believing, their nonbelief, are censured.

How is it that the evangelist, who intends to recount for all generations of the Church some of the principal appearances of the Risen One, noted in each of these appearances that the followers of Jesus did not believe and that in the last appearance the disbelief is blasted by a severe reproof of the Lord? What kind of disbelief are we talking about?

"He took them to task for their disbelief and their stubbornness, since they had put no faith in those who had seen him after he had been raised" (v. 14).

This is the disbelief typical of a hard, sclerotic, rigid heart. The opposite of such disbelief is a heart which is docile, ready, attentive to the signs of God; it is the heart which gives full loving attention to whatever God is doing in history. In other words, it is an inclination to be trustful, it is the intimate certainty that the Lord loves us and will manifest himself to us. It is an interior proneness to see the designs of the Father on the road of Jesus.

The rich young man who, after having been looked at with love by Jesus, went away from him saddened by his words, because he had many possessions (Mark 10:17-22), lacked that kind of inclination. He had a desire to know and yet he was lacking in docility, loving attention, confidence that Jesus would show himself to him more clearly.

This incident shows in a positive way the importance of accepting whatever the Lord tells us and suggests to us, the importance of disposing ourselves to have confidence in the mystery of God. Without such confident expectation, our act of faith remains fragile and ineffectual.

But where does the nourishment for this inclination of the heart come from so that the presence of God in our lives, in the life of the church, in history can be noticed? It is nourished by prayer, by *lectio divina*, by the capacity for gratitude.

And so, with the threefold repetition of this first part of the selection before us, namely, "they refused to believe . . . but not even they believed . . . He took them to task for their disbelief," we can ask ourselves:

"And what about us, O Lord? We are not afraid to tell you that we sometimes find ourselves to be like your first disciples. Our faith, in fact, is accompanied sometimes by a weak availability on our part, a rigidity of heart, a hardness, an inability to understand you. Reproach us, too, O Lord, so that our hearts will welcome you! Teach us not to be afraid of our hardness of heart but, by our perseverance in prayer, to take notice of the signs of your presence!"

In silence and prayerful meditation, let us be prompted to ask from Jesus the gift of not resisting his manifestation in us and in our history.

The mandate of Jesus and the signs of the believer

We are now at the main part of the passage: "Jesus told them: 'Go into the whole world and proclaim the good news to all creation' " (v. 15).

These words strike us because during our missionary vigils we have heard them addressed to so many of our friends who have gone out into various parts of the world. They are all the persons who have received in trust the Crucified One and who, because of the mandate of Jesus, have left our diocese to go into foreign countries.

Within a few days the Lord will repeat his mandate to forty-six young deacons whom I will ordain as priests and, some of them, as missionary priests. They will receive the mandate in a solemn way by the imposition of my hands, and I ask you to pray intensely for them.

"Preach the good news" is the fundamental announcement of Jesus, but perhaps it is best not to use the word *preach*, which has a clerical flavor. In fact, it means "shout out the gospel, proclaim it." Shout out is not some simple formula, but the dominion of Christ, the power of him, who died and rose, over the world of today and over my life; shout out about the power that Jesus has to transform the entire universe.

This is the mandate which the Lord entrusts to each of us, and he asks for silence, loving attention, the capacity to listen.

"Grant me, O Lord, the grace to listen to these words and to proclaim your sovereignty in my life, over the world and over all reality."

The sovereignty of Jesus over the world is expressed by five signs which, at first blush, appear strange to us: "Signs like these will accompany those who have professed their faith: they will use my name to expel demons, they will speak entirely new languages, they will be able to handle serpents, they will be able to drink deadly poison without harm, and the sick upon whom they lay their hands will recover" (vv. 17-18).

When I was a young boy and listened to this gospel passage I felt fear inside me because I said to myself, "At this moment I am not able to do such things, which means that I do not have faith!''

Even today, when listening to them again, I experience fear, but my confidence has grown after having learned to see that the signs promised by Jesus are realized in us believers—in you, such great young people whom I have the joy to know. In fact, the ability to endure difficulties, contradictions, criticism, even derision, and to bear these with peace and courage, translates the parable: ''If they can drink such poison, it will not cause them harm.''

The ability to confront the social and cultural complexities of our day without being afraid, without feelings of inferiority, but rather with the certainty that God is always with us, makes us realize the meaning of the words ''they will be able to handle serpents'': they will have no fear of situations which, of themselves, can be disturbing.

The ''signs which will accompany those who believe'' are not directly religious (going to church, praying), but civil, human, and social; they show life in its entirety as a non-violent choice. They express the capacity to face adverse difficulties not by overcoming them in an offensive or polemic way, but in the totality of peace, in peace without arms.

This is also why we see as a remarkable sign in our day vocations to be workers of peace, to choose the meekness of the gospel, not to render evil for evil, not to prepare reprisals against those who offend us or could offend us. This is the new life in Christ, the testimony that Jesus is the Lord of history and the one who gives rise to a generation of new men and women who are marked by peace, who have the capacity of forgiveness starting with the smallest circumstances of life, who do not work by aggression or polemics. They are the signals of a prophecy of peace, of action which neutralizes wars; they are the signals of a prophecy of disarmament, which shows the futility of arms; they are the signs of a confidence in the power of a truth which is pacifying, not bellicose, of a cure for hearts poisoned by violence. Finally, perhaps by recognizing that we do not know how to handle serpents, nor have the courage to drink poison, we will come to know how to be made strong by the peacefulness of Christ, by the power of his cross. That is why we can question ourselves about the signs which accompany those who believe in Jesus by asking ourselves:

Do I return evil for evil, insult for insult, criticism for criticism? Am I sharp with those around me, am I aggressive for fear of receiving the first blow, am I desirous of conquering a situation so as not to be overpowered by it?

Or am I walking around the world with confidence in the power of love, of forgiveness, of peace, of mercy, of evangelical meekness, of God's compassion for people? Am I capable of healing within me—by imposing the hands of love, of charity, of service—the blows of violence which cause destruction in our society by creating generations of persons who are frustrated, bitter, sour, and aggressive one against another? Am I capable of carrying peace, of laying hands on these illnesses and causing them then to heal?

If we can recognize, notwithstanding our weakness and fragility, that any of those signs have been given to us we ought to say:

"Reign in us, O Lord, and give us the grace to proclaim your gospel, to preach your glory."

"He confirmed the message"

Finally, let us briefly meditate on the concluding events described in the third part of the passage: "Then, after speaking to them, the Lord Jesus was taken up into heaven and took his seat at God's right hand. The eleven went forth and preached everywhere. The Lord continued to work with them throughout and confirm the message through the signs which accompanied them" (vv. 19-20).

Here is a complete synopsis of the experience of the primitive Church, which we read extensively about in the Acts of the Apostles. Naturally, it is also a synopsis of everything that we, as successors of that Church, live by and bring to completion: preaching everywhere, to all areas, in every situation, without thinking anyone lost or forgotten by God; the certainty that the Lord works together with us and confirms the word with miracles. They are not miracles of the sun, the moon, and the stars, but the miracles we see in our humble lives, in our capacity to love, to forgive, to become workers of peace.

It is the life of the Church which we have the gift of being able to contemplate and to which we are called at the end of these meetings of the School of the Word which is concluded with this mandate, with this assurance that the Lord is with us, and with a summons to the way which we have carried out up to this point.

Conclusion

I wish to propose two final questions which I consider particularly important.

Have I learned to read the gospel?

In the meetings of the School of the Word have I learned how to perform the *lectio* of the passages, without expecting that everything is going to be told to me by the preacher, but rather by personally extracting from the sacred words of the gospel, which bring us the grace of the Holy Spirit, the word of Jesus, of the apostles and prophets of the primitive Church?

If I can sincerely respond affirmatively I thank the Lord. If, on the contrary, I seem to have still learned only a little, I can ask him to give me a superabundance of his Spirit so that the knowledge of Scriptures will be opened to me.

"You, O risen Lord, who opened your disciples' minds to knowledge of the Scriptures, open also our minds as the fruit of perseverance in the School of the Word."

Have I learned to question the gospel by an analysis of my own situation, by a reflection on my life?

Throughout the seven sessions of these meetings, you have tried to see, by reading passages from Mark, the educational course which the Lord brings to fulfillment for us and the quantum leaps which it implies, the conversions which the Lord asks of us, the jolting moments which the course has proposed and continues to propose to us. We have perceived that only by means of certain courageous quantum leaps, successive jolts, do we reach and understand the power of his mission, gathering it up from the primitive Church so as to carry it forward in our time.

What is it then through me that Jesus is asking of me at this particular moment?

We will have a way to understand it, even if symbolically, because shortly some young people nineteen years old, who have followed during the year a courageous journey, will complete the *redditio symboli*[1] in front of you, as all of us will proclaim that Jesus is the Lord. Their action will help us finally to ask ourselves: Lord, what can I do for you and for your Church? What effort do you want from me so that I can be a worker of peace and bring myself to believe in your presence in my life?

"Grant, O Lord, that we might live this moment of silence in strict communion with ourselves and with you, by taking up one or the other of your words, by reading through them, questioning ourselves, invoking light through the intercession of Mary, the Virgin of faith. Grant us, O Lord, that we may live these last moments gathering from your gospel the joy of living the faith, which through all this year you have wanted to teach us through our course in the School of the Word."

---

[1] *Redditio symboli* refers to a ceremony in which the archbishop presents a personal document embodying the rule of spiritual life to each of the young persons.